Theatre in Tim

Twenty Scenes for the St

Edited by

DOM O'HANLON

methuen | drama

LONDON • NEW YORK • OXFORD • NEW DELHI • SYDNEY

METHUEN DRAMA
Bloomsbury Publishing Plc
50 Bedford Square, London, WC1B 3DP, UK
1385 Broadway, New York, NY 10018, USA

BLOOMSBURY, METHUEN DRAMA and the Methuen Drama
logo are trademarks of Bloomsbury Publishing Plc

First published in Great Britain 2020

Cover design: Louise Dugdale
Design inspired by Scene/Change and the #MISSINGLIVETHEATRE Tape Project

Cover photograph: Graffiti wall © enjoynz/iStock

A catalogue record for this book is available from the British Library.

A catalog record for this book is available from the Library of Congress.

ISBN: PB: 978-1-350-18878-5
ePDF: 978-1-350-18881-5
eBook: 978-1-350-18882-2

Typeset by Mark Heslington Ltd, Scarborough, North Yorkshire, UK
Printed and bound in Great Britain

To find out more about our authors and books visit
www.bloomsbury.com and sign up for our newsletters.

Contents

Introduction: The Drama Species

The present crisis is bigger than the coronavirus epidemic. A crisis is a situation that can't be resolved within the situation where it occurs. That means that society is confronted by itself not by any particular happening within it. This is an age of crisis. Two world wars, Hiroshima, Nagasaki, Auschwitz, cold wars, climate and territory destruction. Existence is a relation between a being and its site. If the being destroys its site it destroys itself. Whatever we do to our environment, nature, weather, animals, they do to us, whatever we do to them we do to ourselves. It's the logic of reality.

Historically money enables society to negotiate within itself. But bankers and financiers now create money that is really debt. The 'price of contemporary money' overburdens society so that the system crashes. The bankers *created* the 2008 financial crash and the public (mostly poor) were forced to bail out the bankers. Under the jiggery-pokery of the economy and industry society is bankrupt and morally twisted. The crisis began to worsen in the 1980s under Thatcherism (drama prefers the spelling 'Thascism'). The normality the state now wants to return to was its disease. Coronavirus is not our 'deadly enemy'. Viruses don't have intentions, they are not even alive, they are parasites within cells and can't replicate without a host. Coronavirus didn't attack us, we invited it in as the guests of the way our economy runs society. Society has become its own enemy. What has this to do with drama? Everything. Drama is not just the house, it is the key to the house

Two and a half thousand years ago Athens created the first urban democracy. It was the first society to accept responsibility for itself. That responsibility meant it needed to understand society and its members. It's why it created the first public theatre. The founding subjects were and are government, community, family, self. They are the sources of the human dilemma. They are bound together by morality. However remote and diverse its plots may be, drama's one subject is justice (just as the object of all jokes is truth). The plot asks what is right and what is wrong – or in social terms what is fitting, seemly, appropriate. Drama is so basic it makes the subjective seem objective. Yet it remains the most subjective conundrum, paradox, in all human societies. Drama binds the ultimate extremes of any possible reality and only tragedy can resolve the paradox.

Drama is about justice. Greek democracy needed to know who decided what is right and what is wrong. It's said the voice of the people is the voice of God. The Greeks brought the audience into the theatre and God onto the stage. God decided right and wrong. But there is a dangerous (often fatal) existential division between religion and politics. God is not a politician but democracy must solve the political problems of the demos, of people and state. The first Greek dramas avoided the problem, partly because the Greeks were blinded by the brilliance of their new invention: drama. But after some time, about the length of a lifetime, the problem couldn't be avoided. The most fundamental of all human crises is the clash between politics and morality. The law can't define justice, justice must first define law. And it would be degenerate to allow aesthetics to define justice, so justice must be the subject of drama and drama's structure must implicitly be derived from justice. The first Greek trilogy is the *Oresteia*, the story of Orestes. It ends with God granting Athens a new law court to replace revenge with justice (really that fobbed off the problem because only the stage, not the law court, can resolve justice or even understand it). The subject was an obsession. Each of the first three great Greek dramatists deal with it. Orestes' father murdered his daughter, Orestes mother murdered his father for murdering her daughter, God ordered Orestes to murder his mother because she murdered his father and when Orestes did God ordered him to be punished for murdering her. Orestes asked why he should be punished for obeying God's order. (Legally he was just acting as God's hangman.) This was the clash between law and justice that the Greeks had created drama to solve. So Euripides wrote another Orestes play. In it, in full hearing of the audience, a character says that God had made a mistake but keep it quiet. With that the first great age of Greek drama came to an end. Gods aren't allowed to make mistakes. The source of morality had been confounded by this clash with politics, the clash democracy had founded theatre to resolve. It meant that the theatre of Dionysus would turn into the Roman arena and its brutality and blood. Actually the Christian religion was the last Greek play – but morally it compromised with political power. That confounded the problem instead of resolving it. It is still unresolved. It is our problem, the problem of all human societies. I read an incident of it today in the morning papers. If from the Greeks till now you trace the contorted inter-development of morality, government, public administration and industry you will find that the failure to resolve the problem is the reason why we are now faced by the coronavirus epidemic. If we don't resolve the problem we will be destroyed by it and our effort to ignore it. Only drama, in some form, can resolve it. That is because drama's foundation subject is justice. All this is brilliantly illustrated by the first play in this book. The whole of drama is there: a victim, a machine, a policeman and a community. As in all drama, the incidentals are there to present the ground problem. Drama is axiomatic with human consciousness. Other animals may be in dramatic events but not in drama. If that were not so our slaughterhouses would be obscene. Drama's subject is justice and we are the drama species.

What is drama? All its different forms and practices reflect a basic drama. The new-born child creates basic drama when its consciousness enters reality. We don't have to learn to be conscious. Consciousness evolved to apperceive reality as the relation of things, cause and effect, as practically and morally consequential. That is an extraordinary ability. (It's why in drama we seek motive.) Consciousness creates meaning – meanings aren't given genetically. A human is a tool that knows itself. It is all a matter of 'stages of development'. Typically it takes a form such as this. We think of walking as going somewhere. An infant doesn't. For it walking is standing still. Then, typically, it 'recalls' that its hands and arms can reach. It first moves as a four-legged animal. It learns that it is in a complexity of situations of learnt and imposed meanings. There is a boundary to experience. Later in a shock it learns the boundary is death and looks for a door in the boundary. Hence drama. Drama walks on the boundary – that is why even the child assesses things as comedy and tragedy. The child's conception of tragedy lacks only money. These things are not genetic, they are learnt with responsibility. Our life *is* this play. In the house, kitchen, bedroom, street, the institution, we are in the play. The difference between being in, say, the street and in theatre is that in theatre we dissemble reality in order to find what play our lives are in in the street. To the play it adds the child's pleasure when it learnt, say, to walk. Creativity is in fact dis-assembling. All artists know you can't draw a human face without commenting on it. In the stage play you learn your role. The actor amalgamates his life (the elaborations, processes, I've pointed to) with the life of the character. The actor's life authenticates the characters' 'reality'. Theoretically the character could play the actor. (This would then be impossible only when the actor's performance was inauthentic.) The performance involves (occurs in) two brains: the actor's brain and the spectator's. The spectator's brain is involved in the performance in the way the actor's brain is involved in the character. More exactly, because this is a social discipline the character's brain is involved in the actor's brain. In fact three brains are involved: the Greeks created the stage to be a public brain, a social reality for actor and spectator to enter. (As a church is a place said to be inhabited by God.) This isn't a municipal abstract pretence, the site is cathected simply *by* being the pretence of 'the site of a social brain' – as a saw is inherent in the table it makes. We think imagination escapes the bounds of reality but imagination is the only way we can 'enter' the complexity of the facts of reality. All other facts are mechanical. It means that only drama makes us human. It does this not abstractly but by confronting us and our situation in the intimate and the universal, the private and the ontological.

I am introducing a book about modern drama but write about Greek drama. Why? It seems surprising. I do it to stress the vital function of drama. It is the moral centre of humanness and is essential to our survival. Morality is the greatest evolutionary device. We cannot survive without it and drama is morality's centre.

Read this story. 'The prison warder serves the condemned his last meal. The condemned refuses to eat it. Why? Because there is no salt in it. The warder says weep on it.'

The story is the image of our present society. The convict is free not to eat, the warder free to control and contrive. Is that tragedy or farce?

The Greeks constructed tragedy because it's the only way they (and now we) can live with the problem they couldn't solve and we haven't solved. The problem makes us human by our attempts to solve it. This is why we are the drama species. For two and a half thousand years we have sought to solve it. In all that time drama has remained contemporary, even when it was absent from the stage and confined to libraries. We may now be about to destroy it. The economy, market, technology, industry can't solve the problem. They can only tamper with mechanical constructions and contrivances. If we ignored the problem our passions would become feral and our relations pathological. If that happens we could not be able to escape into oblivion but be vegetables that suffer. Tragedy and farce share the same problems. When a sane viable society confronts a tragic situation it may resort to farce as a breathing space that still allows it to reassemble its strength to celebrate the future and trust the practicality of politics. But now we need to understand how the inner contradictions, contortions, of tragedy are comic. If it were otherwise we would be the devil's species.

Our crisis is that we no longer know the difference between tragedy and farce. The one subject of all drama is the audience, their lives and society. Drama asks why the audience came to the theatre. That is, what are we doing with our lives? But now we have no drama. In its place we have the entertainment industry. It is part of the industry-finance complex I describe in the first paragraph of this Introduction. Like all modern industries it has the defects of post-enlightenment society. The audience are the entertainment industry's raw material. It exploits and degrades them as other industries exploit and degrade the natural world that is our *only* means of survival. Theatre and politics are essential aspects of one another. This is why the tragedy of our present crises has turned into farce. Inevitably farce has penetrated or threatens to penetrate the institutions of society. Our democracy was already an oligarchy of the rich. Now we elect Trump and Johnson. A few years ago that was unthinkable. Trump doesn't just lie he *is* the lie. So how could he understand himself or what he does? He rants and sneers with virtuosic glibness but is intellectually immobile. He would recommend lavatory cleaner as a prophylactic mouthwash against coronavirus. And Johnson isn't even a politician. He is an Eton wha-wha boy who stands on the sidelines and shouts, 'Come on, chaps and chapesses – we can do it!' They are dangerous men who turn our present tragedy into farce. Farceurs can't control government or run affairs (other than amatory) and when they try to control the social chaos their farce has caused, the farce turns into the politics of fascism. That is a law of politics and drama. It lies before us.

Is the story of the warder and condemned a tragedy or farce?

Uncannily this book presents the whole of theatre's present crisis. The first play in the book is a classical example of the structure of drama. The last play seems to throw everything open again. Its actors and characters move in and out of each other's parts, imagination and reality swap and re-swap their places, and the function of the audience is changed. These two plays illustrate all I've written in this Introduction. This is a book of excerpts but together they have an awesome complexity and completeness. It's like looking at the stars not through a telescope but a microscope. They clarify our situation. We are the constellation.

One line in the book is like a signpost that points at the future and stabs it: 'I worry that we'll fall back into traditional modes of storytelling' (Chris Thorpe, *Manchester*). We must not try to imitate the Greeks or any other drama. (We couldn't even if we tried, the social change is too great.) Even if we got rid of the coronavirus epidemic we wouldn't be cured and we certainly wouldn't be saved. The crisis is unprecedented. Our whole existence – society and culture – are in crisis. Not in an epi-crisis but a mega-crisis. We have to create a new drama or – remember the theatre of the theatre of Dionysus – we will turn into pop-barbarism.

The story of the warder and the convict shakes the whole of the entertainment industry – even a skeleton would shiver.

Stay awake all night and think about the story. Can you tell if it's tragedy or farce?

On its last day on earth must the human race go on hunger strike to prove it's human?

Don't weep. Create the new drama.

Edward Bond
August 2020

https://edwardbonddrama.org

* * *

Excerpt: *The Shoe Thief* by Edward Bond

The Shoe Thief is the second play in a trilogy about crises. It deals with coming social collapse. *Dea*, the first play is about the ideological distortions of morality. The last play, *The Rust Coat*, is set in a time after a series of crises in which cause and effect has broken down in both objectivity and subjectivity. The first two plays were written before the present crisis. The third play is still being written. The trilogy dramatises the arguments in the Introduction.

Three

Leonard, *twenties*

Grace, *his wife, twenties*

The flat. Evening. Low light. **L** *half-dozes in an upright chair at the end of the empty table. Silence. A noise off.* **G** *comes in. She wears outdoor clothes. She carries a largish supermarket carrier with a garish advertising image on the sides. She sees* **L**.

G I let myself in.

L *stands. Stays at the chair.* **L** *and* **G** *look at each other.*

G I should have told you I was coming

L How are you? Where d'you live now?

G Im all right. Are you?

L Yes.

G I live on the other side of the city. I rent a bedsit. Its quite comfortable. (*She comes to the table and stands her bag on it.*) You look well.

L Why've you come? – Sit down. (**G** *doesn't sit.*)

G D'you live on your own?

L Yes.

G Ive come to collect a few things. Clothes and –. You'll be glad to get rid of them.

L (*slight pause*) No. They're not in the way.

G Well. I should have warned you.

L Sit down. I kept all your stuff. Its in the cupboard.

G *sits. She doesn't bring the bag nearer to her. She puts her forearms on the table-top.*

L What's the matter? (**G** *shrugs slightly.*) What happened in the end? I didn't try to find out. I'd've had to go back up.

Silence. **G** *puts keys on the table.*

G Im returning your keys.

L Ta.

G What I don't take you can throw out. I just need a few bits . . . I never imagined one day I'd sit here like this. (*Slight pause.*) The first thing I do when I get here is lie. I didn't come to collect my things. Anything of the past. It was an excuse. I have to finish with that. Nothing's gone right since then. I should keep it all to myself. Not come and chatter. Waste your time.

L *comes a few paces closer to her and stops.*

G I do everything wrong these days.

L Don't blame yourself for what happened. You did what she wanted you to do.

G (*silence*) Yes. I said I would. I tried to move her nearer the edge. Make it easier for when she died – just push her over the – not drag. When I touched her I felt she was happy. Her whole body was happy. It was wonderful. Id never felt that in my own body. She said her baby – it laughed. It was happy to be coming in the world. She was killing it. She called me daughter. You'd run off. Shouted you wouldn't do it. I'd said I would. She was dying and I'd given her something at last – something of her own. (*Sits up. Hugs herself.*) I saw it in my head. – She was standing in the street – holding out her coffin like a begging bowl for me to put something in. No one had ever given her anything. She was afraid I'd change my –. Quick quick – she knew I was already changing – get me to the edge – you wont have to carry me – push me off the – you promised. She patted my arm. Like being stroked by a claw. I go over and over it in my –. She pushed herself up the – with her walking stick. I wouldn't – she knew. All her life nothing. (*Tries to control herself.*) I saw it. Nothing – swallowed up by the sky. I pushed her away – she howled like the baby in her –. Wait I'll fetch him – bring him back to – I'll make you – I knew you wouldn't – you'd said no – I watched you go down the – I didn't even call – please let her die thinking I'll come back – fetching you to –. She was writhing on the – trying to hold on to the dirt – like an animal in human rags – it was a relief to look at it – I couldn't see the nothing she'd lived in all her life. I go over and over it. I was hated by a dying woman. How can you be so lonely?

Silence.

L I shouldn't have built the house.

G I went to her hut. Lived there a year. In the mountain it was quiet. I managed it. I did well. Pretended I talked to her. 'Look Im sweeping your floor. Being useful. Looking after your place like a daughter.' Making up for what I didn't do. There were cracks in the walls between the –. I began to think they were eyes looking at me. They were crying her tears. In the mountain you get –. Water dripping from the holes making puddles on the – I saw myself in her tears. I hadn't seen myself for so long. I left. I left her when she was dying so she'd expect me to leave again. I brought that down with me. I live with it in my bedsit. What's the difference between a bedsit and a hut?

L (*quiet*) What did . . .?

G (*not having heard*) Sorry?

L Was anyone there to help when – throw her from the cliff –?

G I don't know. – Only the blind boy. He couldn't.

L Then she killed herself? Is that it? Threw herself down with the baby, to have something not nothing.

G I'll get my things. Pretend that's why I came here. If I get that right perhaps I can pretend I understand the rest.

G *stands. For a moment she wanders vaguely.*

G I've forgotten where the door is . . .

L *stands. Goes to the door. Turns on the light.*

G Yes. (*Pause. She laughs a little.*) I remember something. (*Half-apology.*) It was in the hut. I couldn't leave it. No one would steal it. But it seemed wrong. The hut was damp. Rats came in out of the cold.

G *gives* **L** *her bag. Goes out through the door.* **L** *takes out from the bag a folded linen sheet. He stares at it. Undoes it a little. It is dirty. Damp stains. Some of the stains mark out a grid pattern of the folds. He stares at it uncertain. Touches the surface with one hand. Takes the sheet to his chair. Hangs it on the back. It partly unravels, hangs down. Damp sticks some of the clumps together. Ragged tears where rats pulled at it to eat. Silence.*

G *comes back. She is calmer. She has the bag. It bulges.*

G I feel better now Ive been here. Given it to you. Cant keep it. Its too big for a bedsit. (*No response.*) You know its her sheet? From the meal.

L Thank you.

G Im sorry I spoke so much.

L No.

G (*looks at the sheet*) I didn't know it was in that state. I never touched it. Its as she left it.

L I should have talked to her. Answered her questions. Not leave you with her.

G I'd promised her. Let's not keep asking –

L Questions have to be asked. She told me what she needed. Id liked to ask the baby what it wanted. Die with its mother – or?

G Lets leave it.

L (*nods at sheet*) Its right you brought it. Im glad Ive seen it. Tomorrow it can go in the dustbin. – The curfew's started. The mobs'll be on the streets. Shouting. Blowing their whistles. They'll take your bag.

G Is it so late? I spoke too much.

Slight pause.

L If I asked the baby it would say it wanted to learn to climb cliffs.

G (*pause*) Why do the police let the crowds on the streets? A curfew. The streets are supposed to be empty. They have a new game. If one street catches someone from another street they throw them out on the road. The traffic runs over them. The women get drunk and piss on the blood to wash it away.

L One day the shouting will stop and they'll miss it, be sorry.

L *goes to the door.*

L Come on. (*Stops in the doorway.*) You can't go out now. Is too late.

G *puts her bag on the table.*

G (*speaks quietly*) But why do the crowds –

L The streets are the edge. They don't know it. They don't know who they are, where they are, where they came from or what a question is. They're like the dead who get drunk to feel alive. They yell. Its their democracy freedom party-time. Entertainment. Nothing works anymore. There'll be riots, street war. It'll solve nothing. It'll be too late. Then a disease will break out in the debris, then a disease and another disease. Then it'll go quiet. No yells. They'll walk passed the bodies in the streets and not notice them. Children wont ask how to climb cliffs anymore. Reality's grown sterile. When that happens they'll walk on top of the dead piled on street corners and not see them.

L *and* **G** *go through the door. They don't touch. The sheet is on the back of the chair. The bag and keys on the table.*

Theatre in Times of Crisis

On 12 March 2020 theatres across New York including Broadway went dark. In the UK, government confusion over official guidance led to theatres falling dark on 16 March across the country, plunging the theatre industry into chaos. Plays that were in performance were told they were now closed. Plays that were in previews never had the chance to open to the press. Plays that were in rehearsal never got to move into the theatre. Plays that were on the page never managed to rise to their feet.

The Covid-19 crisis is unlike anything experienced in modern times. Global economies ground to a halt almost overnight. Citizens faced lockdowns in their homes. All around the world governments flanked by scientists and advisors were clearly working on the back foot, attempting to appease citizens with contradictory advice. Slogans were designed to 'brand' the crisis in a certain framework and health workers and key workers became more relied upon than ever before.

After weeks of campaigning and lobbying for clarity on the dire situation the theatre industry found itself in, the UK's Conservative government finally issued the news that a financial package of £1.57 billion was being made available for cultural institutions to 'help them stay afloat while their doors are closed'. Proudly called 'the biggest ever one-off investment in UK culture' the money was designed to 'provide a lifeline to vital cultural and heritage organisations across the country hit hard by the pandemic'. Whilst the news was of course welcome across the sector, at the time of writing no clarity has been given over how this money will be distributed and exactly who it will benefit. The government went on to approve the re-opening of theatres from 1 August 2020, only if social distancing measures were put into practice – something that almost all saw to be an impossible commercial task with reduced capacity audiences. The Broadway League in New York announced that live performances wouldn't be able to begin until January 2021 at the earliest, with producers such as Cameron Mackintosh signalling that his West End productions would follow suit, remaining closed until 2021.

I sincerely hope that you're reading this book at a time in the future when theatres around the world are back open and some sense of 'normalcy' has been restored. Perhaps it's not the same normal we were familiar with before March 2020; perhaps it is in fact the often cited 'new normal' that politicians were preparing us all to accept. Either way, I hope that this book acts as a snapshot and documentation of a crisis that affected people around the globe, across different jobs, industries and backgrounds yet one that disproportionally affected those most vulnerable in society.

'Crisis' is a buzzword within theatre even in normal times and has come to mean many things to many people. Critically, it can be used when describing structure, often in place of the word 'climax'. In ordinary parlance it is frequently overused to describe everything from a trivial inconvenience to a horrendous accident, rending the word itself somewhat meaningless in terms of relative scale.

This book was born out of the idea that this particular moment of time needed to be captured in written form, and who better to do that than twenty of the world's finest playwrights? I have often found that conversations with writers about their work and practice during 'normal' times often raises this sense that theatre has the ability to deal with difficult moments in the most effective ways. Theatre, as these examples all show, has a profound, unique and uncompromising way of moving its audience and placing them in a specific moment, primarily through shared feeling and a sense of collective breath. With live events and theatre shut down for, at the time of writing, the foreseeable ten months, there was painful irony in the fact that a space for collective healing, discussion, education and togetherness was being denied to us at a time where we need it most.

Rather than commission rapid responses to this time or quick pieces, I was more interested in the writers' previous work speaking for itself, outside of the specific context for which it was written. I was interested in the idea of 'crisis' and how that manifests on stage amongst different circumstances and through a range of characters, experiences and situations. Writers were given a scant brief in terms of selecting their own work – some found this an immediate, easy task, others offered up a number of different suggestions each as relevant as the last before finally settling on one extract.

What strikes me looking at this collection of twenty scenes is how different they are in terms of crises that they represent. The majority of these plays have been written in the past decade and so themselves reflect anxieties of everything from the post-9/11 period to the War on Terror and contemporary issues including police brutality that continue to be discussed on stages around the world.

The first time I read Chris Thorpe's extract from *Manchester* from *The Mysteries*, I felt a shiver down my spine. Its ability to speak to a collective moment of terror yet extend beyond the specific proves exactly why theatre as a form is unique. I could feel how it connected to Simon Stephens's chosen scene from *Motortown* and again to Chris Shinn's post-9/11 play *Where Do We Live*, in reflecting wider moments of global crisis in highly personal and singular moments and situations.

Alistair McDowall's extract from *X* explores crisis in form in a way that is able to transcend the structural confines of theatre itself yet manages to resonate with both Morgan Lloyd Malcolm's *Emilia* and Laura Wade's *The Watsons* where characters 'step out' of a moment and question not just the situation they are in but find the crisis existential and direct. They seem in dialogue with Tim Crouch's scene from *Adler & Gibb*, equally boundary-pushing in terms of form, captured here in a transcendent moment of imitation and abstraction. As the central character of Anne Washburn's *The Internationalist* shows, sometimes these moments are impossible to understand and comprehend. Together they present complex feelings that I think many faced with lockdown could relate to.

Tanika Gupta, Frances Ya-Chu Cowhig and Hannah Khalil each take historical moments that in turn find resonate points of crises and manage to extend these beyond the frame of the storytelling into a wider frame that makes us question character, plot and historical truth. Along with Sudha Bhuchar's powerful *Child of the Divide* they show how theatre can explore stories rooted in history and real life that should encourage the education and understanding of what has happened, and indeed is still happening, in communities and countries all over the world.

James Graham, Lucy Prebble and Vinay Patel offer couples facing their own moments of intense crisis that manage to speak within and beyond their immediate relationships to offer authentic voices in extreme environments. Zoe Cooper's monologue from *Jess and Joe Forever* offers a beautiful and powerful crisis of character that compounds metaphor and shows a resolute moment of clarity and strength. That intimacy is echoed in Gurpreet Kaur Bhatti's *A Kind of People* as honest conversations stir feelings and discussions that compound a number of different crises that occur throughout daily discourse, an idea that continues into Inua Ellams's scene from *Barber Shop Chronicles* which is cross-generational and multi-faceted in terms of the questions and issues it presents an audience.

Philip Ridley's landmark play *The Pitchfork Disney* broke all the rules when it premiered. I'm delighted to see that spirit continue into Phil's response to the theme which offers an artist's view of the questions through fragments that individually stir powerful feelings and collectively sear into your soul and demand repeated study.

Mojisola Adebayo's play *The Interrogation of Sandra Bland* is included here in its entirety. A short play originally written in 2017, its relevance is felt again now as a direct response to the Black Lives Matter movement and the events occurring around the world following the murder of George Floyd in Minneapolis, Minnesota on 25 May 2020. Verbatim and urgent, its point of crisis is clear, and it is described by the author as 'a play of what is happening now and what must stop happening, forever'.

Connecting with each playwright I conducted a number of interviews via Zoom, software which overnight became the main method for professional communication. Zoom plays, Zoom monologues and Zoom readings have become the norm over the past four months and when the story is told of how we collectively overcame this crisis, most probably by one or more of these inspiring writers, Zoom will no doubt feature as a central character. Keeping questions simple and related to the text each had chosen I was interested in their responses to the wider topics and the immediate problems facing the theatre industry and the creation of new work. Whilst there was a unanimous response to the need for government intervention in the arts, something that thankfully came mid-way through creating this book, responses to the nature of crisis in theatre and how its function in drama were wide and conflicting.

The point of this brief wasn't to look back through plays and pull out moments of 'doom and gloom' or indeed try and find moments on stage that point to this specific situation, a pandemic or global shutdown. Instead the scenes consider the word 'crisis' in a much broader sense, as a narrative or structural point of contact within drama. The idea being that theatre of differing forms written at different periods of time can each offer methods of understanding and coping within present situations. They each demonstrate theatre's ability to speak to crises on multiple levels which in turn give audiences the tools and abilities to cope in different ways.

Edward Bond's 'moment of clarity' came up in multiple interviews with authors who cited his anecdote about being involved in a car crash. In that moment, as the car span out of control he entered a moment of increased clarity which he described as 'accident' or 'emergency' time. As Simon Stephens in his interview later in this book comments, 'it's in an emergency that our bodies are more alert, it's in emergency or crisis when our synapses are firing and our pores are more open, our brains are awake'. These twenty scenes each show that specific moment of crisis and present a clarity in a manner that only theatre can achieve. Together they show that in this deep moment of global crises we need theatre now more than even before.

Dom O'Hanlon
Senior Commissioning Editor, Methuen Drama
July 2020

MISSING / LIVE / THEATRE /

Scene/Change #MISSINGLIVETHEATRE Tape Action

Scene/Change is a collective of stage designers driving positive change for theatre and the design community through art, advocacy and action.

From early on in the Covid-19 lockdown, Scene/Change was uncomfortably aware of the negative visual imagery and sadness around closed theatres. Buildings usually teeming with life were dark and bleak. Some were even shut away behind hazard tape like danger zones, to prevent them inadvertently becoming places of gathering.

Scene/Change wanted to wrap our theatres in a positive message, to send out a message of hope and visibility to the industry and the millions of audience members, and to place the positive role of design at the centre of our recovery.

Working with designers, venues and production photographers across the UK, specially printed #MISSINGLIVETHEATRE pink barrier tape was used to wrap and decorate theatres all over the country in dynamic and eye-catching ways.

This heartfelt phrase became playful and subversive when printed onto hazard tape. Here was a declaration of affection, wrapping these buildings with ribbons and bows, and also the visual language of a serious incident, a place of loss.

It was a way to publicly celebrate these buildings at the heart of our cultural life and communities – from the National Theatre to local arts centres and amateur companies – while also highlighting the ongoing financial and employment crisis as they remained closed.

The tape installations stayed at each theatre for one week before the tape was recycled and sent to another venue to use. Throughout July 2020, over 400 designers and volunteers worked with 20 kilometres of tape and 110 venues from Plymouth to Inverness and Belfast to Norwich, to create a truly national event.

The #MISSINGLIVETHEATRE tape project ran for just three weeks but for many, the images of the installations remain the definitive visual record of the theatre industry at the time.

www.scene-change.com
Instagram and Twitter @_scene_change

#SCENECHANGE

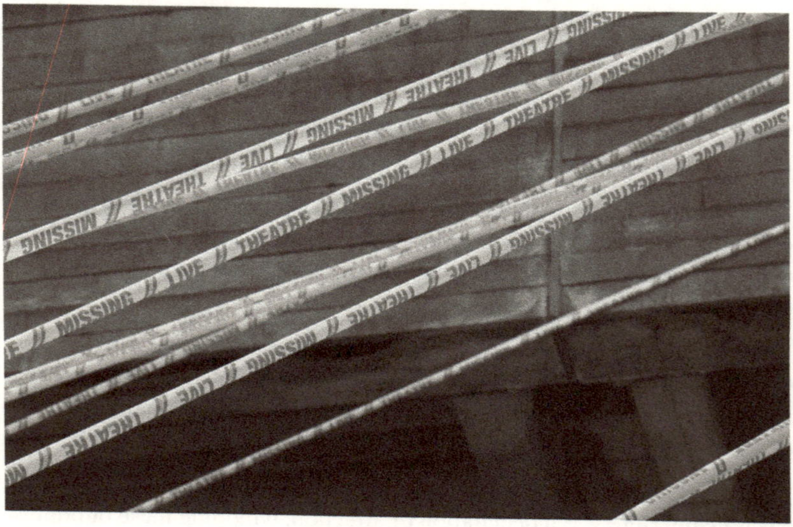

The Interrogation of Sandra Bland

Mojisola Adebayo

Mojisola Adebayo is a playwright, performer, director, producer, workshop facilitator and lecturer. She has a BA in Drama and Theatre Arts, an MA in Physical Theatre and her PhD is entitled *Afriquia Theatre: Creating Black Queer Ubuntu Through Performance* (Goldsmiths, Royal Holloway and Queen Mary, University of London). Mojisola trained extensively with Augusto Boal and is an international specialist in Theatre of the Oppressed, often working in locations of crisis and conflict. She has worked in theatre, radio and television, on four continents, over the past twenty-five years, performing in over fifty productions, writing, devising and directing over thirty plays, and leading countless workshops, from Antarctica to Zimbabwe. Her own authored plays include *Moj of the Antarctic: An African Odyssey* (Lyric Hammersmith and Ovalhouse, London), *Muhammad Ali and Me* (Ovalhouse, Albany Theatre, London and UK touring), *48 Minutes for Palestine* (Ashtar Theatre and international touring), *Desert Boy* (Albany Theatre, London and UK touring), *The Listeners* (Pegasus Theatre, Oxford), *I Stand Corrected* (Artscape, Ovalhouse, London and international touring) and *The Interrogation of Sandra Bland* (Bush Theatre, London). Her publications include *Mojisola Adebayo: Plays One* (Oberon Books), *48 Minutes for Palestine* in *Theatre in Pieces* (Methuen Drama), *The Interrogation of Sandra Bland* in *Black Lives, Black Words* (Oberon Books) and *The Theatre for Development Handbook* (Pan, co-written with John Martin and Manisha Mehta) as well as academic chapters published by Methuen Drama, Palgrave Macmillan and various journals. Mojisola Adebayo is a Fellow of the Royal Society of Literature; an Associate Artist with Pan Arts, Building the Anti-Racist Classroom Collective and Black Lives, Black Words; an Honorary Fellow of Rose Bruford College, a Visiting Lecturer at Goldsmiths and a Lecturer at Queen Mary, University of London. She has recently been awarded a Fellowship at Potsdam University (Germany). *Wind/Rush Generations* and her new play *STARS* both open in 2021. Mojisola is currently writing *Family Tree*, commissioned by Matthew Xia of Actors Touring Company and Young Vic. See **www.mojisolaadebayo.co.uk** for more.

What does the word 'crisis' mean to you in a theatrical sense?

My teacher and mentor Augusto Boal often referred to the kind of crisis that we explore in Theatre of the Oppressed. Augusto referred to it as 'Chinese crisis', inspired by the Mandarin symbols for crisis which are both danger and opportunity. Augusto didn't speak Mandarin and neither do I but the point has always stayed with me: that in a Forum Theatre play in particular, we see our protagonist reach a point where there is both great danger and great opportunity for something to change, personally and politically.

How do you feel theatre has the ability to represent/respond to global crises?

Theatre for me is the art of human relationships in space – in the now, it is the art of being human on planet earth – together, it is the art of dialogue in the sense of working things out with one another (with or without words), it is the art of *ubuntu* – to quote the Southern African philosophy of humanity, empathy, understanding and compassion which broadly means, I am me through you and you are you through me or to quote Muhammad Ali: 'Me, We'. So because of all that theatre is at its core, I feel it is *the* most necessary art form for understanding, questioning and coming up with solutions for problems that human beings have created on this planet.

Why did you pick this specific scene? What is this scene doing at this point of the play?

When you kindly asked me to share a scene of crisis, I thought immediately of *The Interrogation of Sandra Bland*. It is both a scene and a play that represents a black woman at a point of intense crisis, of danger and opportunity (to refer to Boal and the Mandarin symbols for crisis mentioned above). The danger is that Sandra Bland will die a brutal death in a police cell. The opportunity is that she will win her battle with an unjust police officer. The police officer, Encinia, is also in great danger of a kind; he is in danger of betraying his own humanity and hers, in danger of being the worst of whiteness and he has an opportunity to be his best self and to undo his racism and sexism. In turn, as performers and participants in the drama, we are all forced to consider our position in relation to Sandra Bland, how far we are victims and survivors of the danger of racism, and what power and privilege we can assert, in this great opportunity at this time in history to end discrimination. As a black woman, I know I could have been in Sandra Bland's shoes, in Sandra Bland's car. For a white person reading or participating in the play (even silently listening) they are also forced to consider their position in all this, how whiteness implicates them in this drama. The play demands that whatever the colour of your skin, you ask yourself, could I have been Sandra Bland, and if yes, how will I fight on and also protect myself and heal from racism, and if I could not have been Sandra Bland, then what am I going to do to betray the racism and sexism that leads to the conclusion of the scene? How will I be, to quote Noel Ignatiev and John Garvey, a 'race traitor'; i.e. what will I do to dismantle the structures of white supremacist power that have given me this position of privilege? You are either part of the solution or part of the problem. You are either a supporter of white power or you are a traitor to it. You either are Sandra Bland, live in active *daily* solidarity with Sandra Bland or you are, and you are with, Encinia. The time for silence is over. The time for complicity is over. The time for apathy is over. There was indeed never meant to be a time for any of it. Enough.

How does this scene speak beyond the wider context of the play?

The scene is a play that speaks to and from the Black Lives Matter movement, it is verbatim and urgent, it is a play of what is happening now and what must stop happening, forever. It is a play that I would like my grandchildren not to understand, because I want them to be confused when I tell them what racism was, because it is a strange idea of the past, the past, the past.

As a writer, do you feel a point of crisis is always necessary in a play to create/maintain/sustain drama?

Yes. Crisis is a point of high stakes tension, where the story could go one way or another, where the audience cannot predict the outcome, and where the audience are invested in the decisions of the characters, yes.

Does theatre as a form allow for a more effective exploration of crisis in terms of what can be explored, presented and communicated to an audience, in relation to other creative forms?

For me, theatre has a unique power and possibility because it is the art of art forms. All art forms can be part of theatre (music, animation, light, sound, digital arts, circus, literature, dance, poetry, painting, puppetry, sculpture, cabaret, ritual, film and so on). Yet you can also make theatre with nothing but people in space and time, stripped bare, without even a word spoken . . . but what you have got to have is a want, a deep and urgent want that is deferred, or has an obstacle before it, or someone else's want blocking it – conflict and this conflict inevitably leads to some kind of crisis, internal or external, some point where things could go one way or another, to be or not to be, to live or to die, to arrest her or let her go free . . .

What do you feel is the biggest threat to the creation of new drama and plays given the current global crisis? Do we need theatre now more than ever?

I feel the biggest threat to theatre is that we forget that theatre is happening in every moment, in living, in being in relation, and theatre can happen in your living room or under a tree, we can enjoy all the aesthetic wealth and craft of course, we can enjoy being close and sweaty in rooms together but fundamentally we don't need buildings, we can do it without funding . . . We just need to be alive. If Covid-19 were to close every theatre building, if all the money dried up, even if the playwrights stopped writing and the actors stopped training, theatre would still be in us, because it is the art of being us, in relation to each other, the art of understanding each other; all we need is to be alive. White people are still killing black people because of racism, capitalist nations destroying eco-systems, more people trafficked in slavery today than during the transatlantic slave trade, thousands of refugees being allowed to drown in the sea . . . those are threats, that is crisis. Theatre people need to stop fretting about the future of theatre and focus on what it is for. Theatre was in us before humans scrawled symbols on slates that became words and it will go on being, even if no one writes another word. And of course we will go on writing plays . . . the point is what will our plays do?

***The Interrogation of Sandra Bland* premiered at the Bush Theatre, London on 24 March 2017 with the following creative team:**

Writer/Dramaturg Mojisola Adebayo
Director Omar Elerian
Assistant Director (Community Chorus) Mojisola Adebayo
Performers all playing Sandra Bland:
Sheila Atim
Akiya Henry
Judith Jacobs
Sapphire Joy
Sarah Niles
Juliet Okotie
Indra Ové
Plus a large community cast of women all playing Sandra Bland
Performer (playing Brian Encinia) John Last
Performer (playing Female Officer) Ruth Minkley

Background

In June 2016, Simeilia Hodge-Dallaway of Artistic Directors of the Future (ADF) invited me and several other black playwrights to write a fifteen-minute play for the first Black Lives, Black Words event in London, at the Bush Theatre. The brief was to respond to the question, 'Do black lives matter today?' I felt both overwhelmed and humbled at the gravity of the task. I had no idea where to begin. Then I remembered Sandra Bland, having followed (like so many of us have done) an appalling online trail of humiliations and violations of our African kin, across the Atlantic and on our own European island, Britain. I remembered how awed I was by Sandra Bland during the roadside interrogation that led to her brutal arrest and eventual death by hanging in police custody, recorded on the dashboard camera of the police car that pulled her over. I was moved by Sandra Bland's courage, her wit, intelligence, integrity, strength, tenacity and helplessness in the face of the arresting police officer. The interrogation also struck me as a horribly gripping and dramatic 'scene' that escalates with devastating dramaturgical effect. I thought I could not write anything more compelling or important than this. I could not write anything that demonstrates more acutely the various levels of anti-black racism and white supremacist mentality in action than this. However, I did not want to just re-stage the real-life scene. Anyone can click on YouTube to see it. I have no taste for verbatim plays that only translate reality rather than transport the audience imaginatively. I want theatre to do something that a web page, a news clip or a mainstream documentary cannot do. Then an idea came to me. Let us take the words of Sandra Bland and have them spoken by one hundred black women who all play her. Sandra Bland was evidently a brilliant woman; she was sharp, clever, funny, brave, dignified, talented and educated. There was no one like her and her life can never be replaced. Yet any one of us black women could have been in Sandra Bland's shoes. My idea in having Sandra Bland played by a huge chorus of black women is that she is shown as an every-black-woman. We elevate Sandra Bland's status and the status of all black people who have faced similar situations, through the amplification of the voice, a magnification of the struggle. The performance is in this way a theatrical memorial to Sandra Bland and whom she represents. This is a spoken requiem. Furthermore, by magnifying and illuminating the encounter, audiences are encouraged to investigate the scene and interrogate the interrogation. Lastly, in this performance I want to offer an opportunity for a civic ritual through which as many of us as possible can creatively participate in the Black Lives Matter movement. So I sat down at my desk, watched the online clip over and again, and transcribed the roadside interrogation and arrest of Sandra Bland by state trooper Brian Encinia on the 10 July 2015, in Waller County, Texas, USA.

We chose not to stage the piece as planned in 2016 as the legal proceedings were still in process. Moreover, I really wanted Sandra Bland's family to give us their blessing for the performance to go ahead. We tried, but ADF were not able to reach the family. This raises a question about the ethics of going ahead with the staging; for me, however, this question was answered by the fact that Sandra Bland was herself an active part of the Black Lives Matter movement. For example, she regularly addressed and encouraged her 'kings and queens' in her online broadcasts 'Sandy Speaks', speaking to issues of racism and uplifting people who listened. Importantly, Bland specifically called to a passer-by filming her arrest, 'Thank you for recording! Thank you.' Lastly, the dash cam recording is already in the public domain. I hoped that, as we approached the first staging of *The Interrogation of Sandra Bland* at the Bush Theatre on 24 March 2017, we had, in some way, Sandra Bland's own spiritual and political blessing for her unaltered recorded words to be heard and multiplied, loud and clear, with full emotional commitment, in the theatre. If it was me, I would want people to know what happened and how. This was another way of recording and hopefully making something beautiful out of the brutal; something revolutionary out of the revolting abuse of life. Sandra Bland was arrested when she was on her own and she died in a police cell. The amplification of her voice in the staging becomes a collective gesture of solidarity and support. We said to ourselves: Sandra Bland's voice will not be alone again.

The first performances, directed by the brilliant Omar Elerian, at the Bush Theatre were astonishing. I have worked in theatre for twenty-five years, but I have never experienced anything so powerful. I was shaking. There was a core cast of seven professional black women actors, two white actors playing the police officers and a huge community cast of women from all cultural backgrounds. The actors, community participants and audience members were deeply moved. There was stunned silence at first and then passionate discussion about the work late into the evening. People are still talking about it. All the actors have kept in touch and still have a deep bond over this work. We felt we had done the right thing in going ahead. I have since used the script with students, conference delegates and participants at community and arts events, where the effect has also been very powerfully moving and politically galvanising. We know it works.

Later in 2017, on a trip to work with Dr Ama S. Wray at the University of Wisconsin-Madison, USA, I took a diversion to Chicago and was finally able to meet with one of Sandra Bland's precious sisters, my shero, my queen, Shante Needham. Our introduction was facilitated by the family lawyer Cannon Lambert, to whom I am also sincerely grateful. I was and am so immensely blessed and touched that Shante Needham gave her blessing for the work, after speaking with and on behalf of the family. Thank you all.

We subsequently presented the first US performance of *The Interrogation of Sandra Bland* as part of the Black Lives, Black Words, I AM . . . Fest, curated and directed by the extraordinary Simeilia Hodge-Dallaway and Reginald Edmund, at Goodman Theatre, Chicago on 29 April 2019. The performance was astonishing. A few days later, new evidence was released about Sandra Bland's unjust arrest. It was as if Simeilia and the huge chorus of women in Chicago had summoned up the truth. The fight for justice continues, and so does the life of this play. We will keep on playing, all over the world, until this systemic violence against our people is merely a shameful chapter in history.

I want to extend my huge thanks to all of you who have made and will make this performance happen so powerfully and beautifully. Thank you to the family of Sandra Bland. Thank you to all who have supported this project in every way. Moreover, thank you to our queen, Sandra Bland.

How to stage the play

It is crucial that Sandra Bland is played by a large cast of (preferably one hundred) women, led by black women. I suggest a core group of seven black female professional actors (indicated below as BLAND CORE) plus a large community chorus of culturally diverse women (indicated below as ALL) to play Sandra Bland, plus a white male actor and female actor playing the police officers. This is the concept. In doing this work, on a large scale, but in detail, we are both magnifying Sandra Bland and putting the arrest under a magnifying glass. It must be both a requiem and an uprising, art and activism, a memorial to move the Black Lives Matter movement.

I suggest that the BLAND CORE cast of seven rehearse for one week or more, whatever is possible. The BLAND CORE group of seven can then be joined by the large community chorus of culturally diverse women for shorter periods of rehearsal. At the Bush Theatre in 2017 we rehearsed the chorus for one day. They arrived in the morning, rehearsed with the professional actors all day and then performed in the evening. No one had a script in hand. It is also possible to play the piece without any rehearsal, by projecting the text on a screen, casting it quickly and reading aloud together. This can also be very powerful.

As you will see from the script, some lines are spoken collectively en masse, some lines are taken by one woman, some in pairs, groups and so on. I have suggested numerically where Sandra Bland's lines may be spoken by a solo member of the core (e.g. BLAND ONE), a pair from the core, a grouping or the entire core of seven – indicated by BLAND CORE. ALL means the core plus the community chorus.

Important: unless it says pause, don't. Be tight on cue in Bland's lines: they flow from one mind. Pay attention to Sandra Bland's own striking use of repetition, a kind of call-and- response. This performance is like playing music through words: you have to feel it, you have to listen, deeply. The audience, too, should feel like participants, not mere witnesses, and this sense can guide the quality of playing. Whatever you do, this piece cannot be reduced to a naturalistic staging by three people behind a fourth wall, as that would miss the point entirely. Sandra Bland must be amplified, elevated and magnified, for the reasons I discuss above. There is power in the collective. The words of Encinia, however, are to be spoken by one solitary white male actor, present on stage. He stands behind a microphone on a stand. His voice is the only one that is amplified. There is also a brief exchange with an unnamed female police officer, which should be played by just one white female actor, also physically present, behind a microphone. The piece is technically simple otherwise. There is just a short projection of a statement before and after the performance.

In terms of the actors' playing style, this is a study, an interrogation of an interrogation. As such the text should be spoken with absolute clarity and precision, observing punctuation, including exclamation and question marks. Do not drop a line. The audience must not miss a word unless it is deliberately inaudible. However, there is no need for emotional detachment. Everyone is playing a person. You cannot act a symbol or a function. This is not reading the news; work out what is happening emotionally to the characters and commit to it. It is not, in my opinion, necessary to 'put on' North American accents, unless it feels right to the actors themselves. What is more important is a sense of the African diasporic rhythm and tone that Sandra Bland displays, black musicality in speech; whether this has African-American, Caribbean, African or Black British flavours, to me this does not matter. It is important to the inclusive ethic of the work that people who are D/deaf or hearing impaired are not excluded from the performance, as performers and spectators. Therefore integration of sign languages, sign-language interpretation and or surtitles is encouraged.

The use of / in a line indicates where the next speaking character should inter-cut with their line and dialogue overlaps. BLAND always counts as one character. Overlaps are crucial. Pauses should be observed. It might be of interest to explore stylised movement at points and the use and exchange of looks could be key, but whatever movement there is, like all of the staging, should be kept extremely simple and clear. Do not act out the violence literally. There is no need. Let the words do the work.

Projection on screen:

The Interrogation of Sandra Bland
Dedicated to Sandra Bland (1987–2015)
and all our people who have died in police custody

Encinia Hello, ma'am.

Bland Core Hi . . .

Encinia We're the Texas Highway Patrol and the reason for your stop is because you didn't fail . . . You failed to signal the lane change. You got your driver's licence and insurance with you? (*Beat.*) What's wrong?

Bland One (*faintly*) Nothing's wrong.

Pause of around twenty seconds as he looks at the documents.

Encinia How long have you been in Texas?

Bland Two Just got here yesterday.

Encinia Okay. (*Pause.*) Do you have a driver's licence?

Bland Three Didn't I give you my driver's licence?

Encinia No, ma'am. (**Bland Three** *says something inaudible.*)

Okay. (*Pause.*) Okay. Where you headed to now?

Bland Three *says something casual but inaudible.*

Encinia Okay. You give me a few minutes, all right?

Bland Four All right.

Long pause of approximately five minutes as **Officer Encinia** *goes away and keeps* **Sandra Bland** *waiting in her car. Everybody waits and waits . . . The tension builds during this waiting time. Then he approaches* **Bland** *again.*

Encinia Okay, ma'am. (*Pause.*) You okay?

Bland Five I'm waiting on you

Bland Core You . . .

Bland Five This is your job.

Bland Core I'm waiting on you.

Bland Five When're you going / to let me go?

Encinia I don't know, you seem very irritated.

Bland Six I am.

Bland Six *and* **Seven** I really am.

Bland Six 'Cause I feel like it's crap what I'm getting a ticket for.

Bland Seven I was getting out of your way.

Bland One You were speeding up, tailing me, so I move over and you stop me.

Bland Two So yeah, I am a little irritated, but that doesn't stop you from giving me a ticket, so – (*Inaudible.*)

Bland Core – ticket.

Encinia Are you done?

Bland Three You asked me what was wrong and I told you.

Encinia Okay.

Bland Four So now I'm done, yeah.

Encinia Okay. You mind putting out your cigarette, please?

If you don't mind?

Bland Five I'm in my car, why do I have to put out my cigarette?

Encinia Well, you can step on out now.

Bland Six I don't have to step out of my car.

Encinia Step out of the car.

Bland Seven Why am I . . .

Encinia Step out of the car!

Bland Seven No.

All No.

Bland Seven You don't have the right.

Encinia Step / out of the car!

All You do not have the right to do that . . .

Encinia I do have the right now step out / or I will remove you.

All I refuse to say –

Bland One I refuse to talk to you other than to identify myself / I am getting removed for a failure to signal?

Encinia Step out or I will remove you. Step out or I will remove you. I'm giving you a lawful order. Get out of the car now, or I'm gonna remove you.

Bland Two And I'm calling my lawyer.

Encinia I'm going to yank you out of here. (*Reaches inside the car.*)

Bland Three Okay, you're going to yank me out of my car?

Encinia Get out.

Bland Four Okay, alright.

Encinia (*calling in back-up*) 25–47.

All Let's do this.

Encinia Yeah, we're going to. (*Grabs for* **Bland**.)

Bland Five Don't touch me!

Encinia Get out of the car!

Bland Five, **Six** *and* **Seven** Don't touch me.

All Don't touch me!

Bland Seven I'm not under arrest – you don't have the right to / take me out of the car.

Encinia You are under arrest!

Bland One I'm under arrest?

Bland Two / For what?

Bland Three For what?

Bland Four For what?

Encinia (*to dispatch*) 25–47 County FM 10–98. (*Inaudible.*) Send me another unit. (*To* **Bland**.) Get out of the car! Get out of the car – now!

Bland Five Why am I being apprehended? You're trying to give me a ticket / for failure . . .

Encinia I said get out of the car!

All Why am I being apprehended?

Bland Six / You just opened my car

Bland Core You just opened my car door . . .

Encinia I'm giving you a lawful order. I'm going to drag you out of here.

Bland Seven So you're gon', you're threatening to drag me out of my own car?

Encinia GET OUT OF THE CAR!

Bland One And then you're gonna / stun me?

Encinia (*slow this line right down, non-naturalistically, like slow-motion*) I will light you up! (*As normal.*) Get out!

Bland Two, Three and **Four** Wow.

Encinia Now! (*Pointing stun gun at* **Bland**.)

Bland Five, Six *and* **Seven** Wow.

All Wow. (**Bland** *exits car.*)

Encinia Get out of the car!

Bland One For a failure to signal?

Bland Two *and* **Three** You're doing all of this / for a failure to signal?

Encinia Get over there.

Bland Four *and* **Five** Right. Yeah, yeah, let's take this to court

/ let's do this.

Encinia Go ahead.

Bland Six For a failure to signal?

All Yep, for a failure to signal!

Encinia Get off the phone! / Get off the phone!

Bland Seven I'm not on the phone. / I have a right to record. This is my property.

Encinia Put your phone down. Put your phone down!

Bland Core This is my property.

Bland One Sir?

Encinia Put your phone down, right now! Put your phone down!

Bland *slams phone down on her trunk.*

Bland Two For a fucking failure to signal. My goodness. / Y'all are interesting.

All Very interesting.

Encinia Come over here. Come over here now.

Bland Four You feelin' good about yourself?

Encinia Stand right here. / Stand right there.

Bland Five You feelin' good about yourself? For a failure to signal?

Bland Five *and* **Six** You feel real good about yourself don't you?

All You feel good about yourself don't you?

Encinia Turn around. Turn around. Turn around now. / Put your hands behind your back and turn around.

Bland Seven What, what, why am I being arrested?

Encinia Turn around . . .

Bland One Why can't you . . . Can you tell me why . . .

Encinia I'm giving you a lawful order. I will tell you.

All Why am I being arrested?

Encinia Turn around!

Bland Two Why won't you tell me that part?

Encinia I'm giving you a lawful order. Turn around . . .

Bland Three Why will you not tell me / what's going on?

Encinia You are not complying.

Bland Four I'm not complying 'cause you just pulled me out of my car!

Encinia Turn around!

Bland Five Are you fucking kidding me? This is some bull . . . / You know it is!

Encinia Put your hands behind your back.

Bland Six 'Cause you know this is straight bullshit.

And you're full of shit!

All Full of straight shit!

Bland Six That's all y'all are is some straight scaredy fucking cops. South Carolina got y'all bitch asses scared. That's all it is.

All Fucking scared of a female.

Encinia If you would've just listened.

Bland Seven I was trying to sign the fucking ticket –

All – whatever.

Encinia Stop moving!

Bland One Are you fucking serious?

Encinia Stop moving!

Bland Two Oh I can't wait 'til we go to court.

Bland Two, Three *and* **Four** Oooh I can't wait.

Bland Two, Three, Four, Five *and* **Six** I cannot wait 'til we go to court.

Bland Core I can't waaait!

All Ooooh I can't wait!

Bland Six You want me to sit down now?

Encinia No.

Bland Seven Or are you going to throw me to the floor?

That would make you feel better about yourself?

Encinia Knock it off!

Bland One Nah that would make you feel better about yourself?

Bland Two That would make you feel real good, wouldn't it?

Bland Three Pussy ass.

Bland One, **Two** *and* **Three** Fucking pussy.

Bland Four For a failure to signal you're doing all of this. In little ass Prairie View Texas. My God they, they must have . . .

Encinia You were getting a warning until now you're going to jail.

Bland Five I'm getting a – for what?

Bland Five and **Six** For what?

Encinia You can come read.

Bland Six I'm getting a warning for what?

All For what?!

Encinia Stay right here.

Bland Seven Well, you just pointed me over there!

Encinia I said stay right there.

Bland One Get your fucking mind right. Ooh I swear on my life, y'all are some pussies.

Bland Two A pussy-ass cop, for a fucking signal / you're gonna take me to jail.

Bland Three What a pussy!

Bland Core What a pussy . . . What a p–

Encinia (*either to dispatch, or the officer arriving on scene*) I got her in control she's in some handcuffs.

Bland Four You're about to break my fucking wrist!

Encinia Stop moving.

Bland Five I'm standing still! You keep moving me –

All – goddammit!

Encinia Stay right here. Stand right there.

Bland Six Don't touch me. Fucking pussy – for a traffic ticket.

Doing all this bullshit . . .

All For a traffic ticket . . . (*Short pause then door slams.*)

Encinia Come read right over here. This right here says 'a warning'. You started creating the problems.

Bland Seven You asked me what was wrong! / I'm trying to tell you –

Encinia Do you have anything on your person that's illegal?

Bland One Do I feel like I got anything on me? This a fucking maxi dress.

Encinia I'm gonna remove your, I'm gonna remove your glasses.

Bland Core This a maxi dress. (*Inaudible.*)

Encinia Come on over here.

Bland Two Fucking asshole. For a – you about to break my wrist. Can you stop?! You're about to fucking break my wrist!

All (*stretching the word loudly*) STOP!

Encinia Stop moving! Stop now! Stop it!

All *squeal in pain.*

Female Officer Stop resisting, ma'am.

Encinia If you would stop then I would tell you!

Bland Three (*crying*) For a fucking traffic ticket . . .

Encinia Now stop!

Bland Four (*crying*) You are such a pussy.

Bland Three and **Four** You are such a pussy.

Female Officer No, you are! / You should not be fighting.

Bland Five *and* **Six** (*crying*) For a fucking traffic signal!

Bland Core For a traffic signal.

All For a traffic signal.

Encinia You are yanking around. You are yanking around, when you pull away from me / you're resisting arrest.

Bland Seven (*crying*) This make you feel real good, don't it?

All It make you feel real good, don't it?

Bland Seven A female for a traffic ticket, / for a traffic ticket.

Bland One Don't it make you feel good, Officer Encinia?

Bland Two I know it make you feel real good.

Bland Three You're a real man now.

Bland Four You just slammed me, knocked my head into the ground.

Bland Five I got epilepsy, you motherfucker!

Female Officer (*faintly*) I got it. I got it.

(*To* **Encinia**.) Take care of yourself.

Encinia (*spoken immediately after* **Bland**'*s 'I got epilepsy, you motherfucker!'*) Good. Good.

Bland Six *and* **Seven** Good? / Good?!

Female Officer / You should have thought about it before you started resisting.

Bland One All right, all right, this is real good. Real good for a female, yeah. Y'all strong.

All Y'all real strong. Y'all real strong.

Encinia I want you to wait right here. Wait right here.

Bland Two I can't go anywhere with your fucking knee in my back, duh!

Encinia I'm gon' open your door.

Female Officer Okay.

Encinia (*pause, then to a bystander*) You need to leave! You need to leave! You need to leave!

Time passes. **Bland** *continues crying,* **All** *repeating, 'For a traffic signal, full of shit, really? Really for a traffic signal?', etc., but much of it is inaudible.*

Encinia For a warning, for a warning you're going to jail . . .

Bland Three Whatever

Bland Three *and* **Four** Whatever

Bland Five *and* **Six** Whatever . . .

Encinia For resisting arrest. Stand up.

Bland Six If I could / I can't.

Encinia Okay, roll over.

All I can't even fucking feel my arms!

Encinia Tuck your knee in, tuck your knee in.

Bland Seven (*crying*) Goddamn. I can't. (*Muffled.*)

Encinia Listen, listen: you're going to sit up on your butt.

Bland One (*crying*) You just slammed my head into the ground and / you do not even care about that.

All I can't even hear!

Both officers simultaneously:

Encinia Sit up on your butt.

Female Officer Listen to how he is telling you to get up.

Yes you can.

Bland Three (*crying*) He slammed my fucking head into the ground.

Encinia Sit up on your butt. Sit up on your butt.

Bland Four (*crying*) What the hell?

Encinia Now stand up.

Bland Five (*crying*) All of this for a traffic signal. I swear to God.

Bland Six All of this for a traffic signal. (*Clearly to a bystander recording on their mobile phone.*)

All Thank you for recording!

Bland Core Thank you!

Bland One For a traffic signal – slam me into the ground and everything!

Bland Core Everything!

Bland One I hope y'all feel good.

Encinia This officer saw everything.

Female Officer I saw everything.

Bland Three I'm so glad to put that – you just got on the scene so whatever.

Female Officer I was . . .

Bland Four No you wasn't you were pulling up.

Bland Core No you didn't.

Female Officer No, ma'am.

Bland Five You didn't see everything leading up to it . . .

Female Officer You know what, I'm not talking to you.

Bland Six and **Seven** You don't have to!

Bland One You don't have to . . . (*One by one every woman playing* **Bland** *exits saying, 'You don't have to', each in their own way. This can be in any language. When the last woman has said it,* **Encinia** *says his last line.*)

Encinia 25–47 County. Send me a first-available, for arrest.

Projection:

Three days later, Sandra Bland was found
hanging in her police cell.

The End.

A Kind of People

Gurpreet Kaur Bhatti

Gurpreet Kaur Bhatti writes for stage, screen and radio. Her first play *Behsharam* (*Shameless*) broke box-office records at Soho Theatre and the Birmingham Rep. Behzti (*Dishonour*) was sensationally closed after protests at the Birmingham Rep in December 2004; it won the Susan Smith Blackburn Prize, was translated into French and had sell-out tours in France and Belgium. *Behud* (*Beyond Belief*) was co-produced by Soho Theatre and Belgrade Theatre, Coventry, and was shortlisted for the John Whiting Award. *Khandan* had a sell-out run at the Birmingham Rep before transferring to the Royal Court Theatre. Her latest play *A Kind of People* opened at the Royal Court Downstairs in December 2019.

Other credits include: *Elephant* (Birmingham Rep); *Dishoom* (Rifco/ Watford Palace Theatre); *Fourteen* (Watford Palace Theatre); the feature film *Everywhere and Nowhere*; *DCI Stone* (Radio 4); *Londonee* (Rich Mix); *Dead Meat* (Channel 4); and an adaptation of Ibsen's *An Enemy of the People* (BBC World Service).

Her first collection of plays, *Gurpreet Kaur Bhatti: PLAYS ONE*, is published by Oberon Books.

What does the word 'crisis' mean to you in a theatrical sense?

It is the electric moment in a play when the world starts to crumble, when the characters face the hardest of decisions and the story explodes and travels in a different direction.

How do you feel theatre has the ability to represent/respond to global crises?

Theatre is an artistic response to life. Through live performance it presents the opportunity to provoke and raise difficult questions which hopefully push us to further understand who we are and transcend what we think we know.

What is this scene doing at this point of the play? Why did you pick this specific scene?

Gary has come home on a high. He has walked out of his job after his boss came to his house and was racist and inappropriate. His wife Nicky is unhappy that he has left work because she is worried about how they will cope financially. I chose it because it is a key moment in the action; after this, life will never be the same again for either character.

How does this scene speak beyond the wider context of the play?

It is about a man confronting his truth and being in touch with his authenticity. The character finds the courage to entirely be himself and that presents both risk and challenge for the people around him.

As a writer, do you feel a point of crisis is always necessary in a play to create, maintain or sustain drama?

Yes, some kind of conflict or dramatic tension is needed to propel the action forward. Something that goes beyond the everyday and gives characters dilemmas and choices that an audience can identify with or argue about.

Does theatre as a form allow for a more effective exploration of crisis in terms of what can be explored, presented and communicated to an audience, in relation to other creative forms?

Jatinder Verma says that, 'Theatre is the most thrilling art form because it is the most mortal. From the second you start creating it, you are planning its death.' It only ever really exists when it is live and that in itself is extraordinary, powerful and compelling.

When constructing a play how do you effectively boil down larger global themes that could otherwise be overwhelming for characters within 'their world' so that they can find room to resonate?

Identify your character's need and be brave enough to find the truth of the words and of the specific moment.

What do you feel is the biggest threat to the creation of new drama and plays given the current global crisis? Do we need theatre now more than ever?

This is a terrible and frightening time. To think that a generation of artists may not have access to our stages means that we will be culturally impoverished. There is the danger that theatre becomes increasingly elite and expensive. However, artists will always find a way to create and I believe that theatre will survive because ultimately it is bigger than all of us.

***A Kind of People* premiered at the Royal Court Theatre, London in December 2019**

Gurpreet Kaur Bhatti's play focuses on a group of working-class friends dreaming of a better life for their children and questions the dream of class mobility, and what happens when the odds are stacked against you.

Scene Five

Same day. The flat. **Nicky** *is painting* **Mo***'s face – what she's doing cannot be seen.* **Anjum***'s face is painted like a cat. She fills assorted jam jars with various sweets.*

Mo How's your skin?

Anjum Okay, I think. Though I don't see why you couldn't just buy the branded paints.

Mo Brands won't save the school money. Anyway you haven't come out in a rash, so these are almost definitely non-toxic.

Anjum I'm sure Nicky's got better things to do.

Nicky I don't mind.

Mo When you're faced with a queue of little alpha females demanding to be butterflies, you'll be glad of the practice.

Nicky Done.

Hands **Mo** *mirror. She packs the paints away. As he looks up, we see that she's painted a dog face on him.*

Mo That is very . . . lifelike. It's funny . . . I actually feel . . . canine.

(*To* **Anjum**.) Do you know what I mean?

Anjum No. You're supposed to be helping me fill these jars.

Mo You should be putting two sweets in, not four.

Anjum We're charging a quid per jar.

Mo If people can afford iPhones and PlayStations, they can afford a quid to support the school.

Anjum Still no word from Gary?

Nicky He's not answering his phone. Hopefully he's out celebrating.

Mo He probably wants to tell you in person. If it's good news, and I reckon it will be, Mark's gonna babysit and we're taking you both into town. We'll find one of those rooftop restaurants and rub shoulders with the oligarchs and the Chinese and those bearded bastards from Shoreditch.

Nicky You don't have to.

Mo I need a night out. Waiting for these results is gonna give me a brain haemorrhage.

Nicky It is stressful.

Mo There has to be some sort of test. How else do you separate the men from the boys?

Anjum Girls take the eleven plus too.

Mo It's a metaphor. (*To* **Nicky**.) Zaki needs spoonfeeding.

Did you know in one of the mocks, he left half the multiple-choice questions blank?

Anjum He ran out of time.

Mo Who leaves multiple-choice questions blank? You wouldn't, would you?

Nicky I suppose not.

Anjum How's Ronnie coping?

Nicky Alright.

Mo Well he's clever isn't he? Natural intelligence. Our problem is, Zaki's thick. That's why I keep telling him he has to work twice as hard. I mean the second round's in three weeks and he still hasn't come to terms with apostrophes . . .

Anjum Zaki knows exactly where apostrophes go!

Mo Not after irregular nouns.

Anjum (*to* **Nicky**) He's been sick most mornings.

Nicky Poor thing.

Mo I keep telling him, he's got to develop resilience. We're beginning to suffer now. (*Indicates* **Anjum**.) She's hardly sleeping. And I've got a mouth ulcer the size of a 50p piece. Look . . . (*Starts to show* **Nicky**.)

Anjum She doesn't want to see! (*A beat.*) It doesn't help that you're always shouting.

Mo Not always.

Anjum This morning.

Mo Because he keeps confusing prepositions with fronted adverbials! (*To* **Nicky**.) He knows I just want what's best for him.

Nicky At least we find out soon.

Mo What if Zaki's sick for the second round?

Anjum We're not there yet, Mo.

Mo Well, if he gets through, he's sitting the exam no matter what. Asif's daughter shit herself at the start of the verbal reasoning and she still managed to finish the synonyms and antonyms. (*A beat.*) And he doesn't concentrate. I keep telling him. I bought him that meditation app for £2.99. I could have got a free one, but I chose to pay.

Anjum He did better in the last comprehension.

Mo Better is not good enough. (*A beat.*) Something drastic needs to happen. I could . . . tell him I've got cancer.

Nicky Have you?

Mo No. But if he thinks I have, he might try harder.

Anjum Mo, will you stop!

Mo It'll only be for a week or so, once the exam's out of the way the consultant can give me the all-clear.

Anjum I'm not listening.

Mo He has to want it, Anj. Ronnie wants it, doesn't he?

Nicky I think so.

Anjum Give him a chance!

Mo We've already given him too much. (*To* **Nicky**.) Anything he wants. When I was his age, I was in charge of my dad's stock, jointing chickens, chucking drunks out onto the street.

Anjum That was wrong.

Mo It was a better time.

Anjum It wasn't.

Mark *and* **Gary** *bustle in.* **Gary** *picks* **Nicky** *up, swings her round.*

Mo Somebody's happy.

Gary Happy, oh yes.

Mark You should have seen him. Gary's . . . he's a hero.

Nicky Thank God.

Anjum Congratulations.

Gary I didn't get it.

Nicky What?

Mo Oh, mate, no way.

Nicky Why are you smiling?

Gary Because you're all . . . beautiful.

Nicky Gary?

Mark *takes a packet of fruit sweets from his pocket, shows* **Nicky**.

Mark Got these for Tyler. I thought they might stop him screaming on the way to school.

Gary If my boy wants to scream, let him scream.

Nicky Why didn't you ring me?

Anjum I'm really sorry, Gary.

Gary I don't care.

Mark Victoria's a joker. You know how these people stay. One minute they're round your house necking your last Red Stripe and next they're stabbing you in the back with your own kitchen knife.

Anjum I knew it. Your manager is why a good school is essential. You don't want Ronnie's destiny in hands like hers.

Nicky What do you mean?

Mark She's a racist, Nic. Victoria is a racist.

Silence.

Anjum (*to* **Mo**) Let's go and pick up the boys. (*To* **Nicky**.) Ronnie can come back to ours for dinner. (*Packs up fair stuff in a bag which she takes.*)

Mo Your day will come, brother. (*They exit.*)

Gary I'm living it right now, Mo.

Nicky Thought you said the interview went well.

Gary It did.

Nicky We should have had another practice run. I kept telling you to practise.

Gary It's nothing to do with that. Victoria doesn't think a black man can run a team.

Nicky She said that?

Gary She doesn't have to.

Nicky Go and check Tyler for me, Mark.

Mark *heads out.*

Nicky What did you do exactly?

Gary I told her about herself. If I hadn't spoken up, then she'd carry on like that for the rest of her life and nothing, nothing would change. (*A beat.*) I've realised that I've never had a proper chance. And now, I feel like . . . I'm born again. The boys, all of them, Mark and Si and Chas, they're calling me the don.

Nicky You told me the interview went well.

Gary Because it did.

Nicky Did she give you any reason?

Gary What's she gonna say? That I wore the wrong suit or I couldn't spell thermostat. Whatever it is, it's gonna be a lie.

Nicky Right . . . well, we'll put it behind us and move on.

Gary I walked out, Nic. I'm not going back.

Nicky What? (*A beat.*) You can't leave work!

Gary You saw how she was that night.

Nicky You're punishing us because you felt humiliated.

Gary This is down to her, I pointed certain things out and she's slapped me down.

Nicky But what did she say?

Gary The problem is what she doesn't say, it's what she thinks but leaves out of her sentences.

Nicky Fucking hell, do you realise how paranoid you sound?

Gary It's real.

Nicky Why didn't you chuck her out on Mark's birthday?

Gary Because you wanted me to get this fucking job!

Nicky You took her shit then, why not take it now?

Gary I should never have taken it. I can't go to that place day after day and come home and face Ron and Mia and Ty and have respect for myself.

Nicky Victoria is . . . she's nothing. You concentrate on what's best for you. Forget your pride . . .

Gary My pride means something, it makes me who I am.

Nicky Did you lose it with her?

Gary She was taking the piss.

Nicky Shit.

Gary Aren't I allowed to be angry?

Nicky Listen, Gary, you and me . . . we haven't got a house or savings or all the things you're supposed to. And now, we can't catch up, there's a price to pay. We wasted so much time. Going out, getting high, night after night . . .

Gary That was before the kids.

Nicky And when Ron and Mia were little.

Gary They were the golden days. We saw our mates, ennit.

The kids loved it.

Nicky We never made plans, never thought about getting on.

Gary So?

Nicky I don't want the kids to end up . . . (*Falters.*)

Gary What? Like us? Like me? (*No response.*) So you get Ron into this fancy school, and then what?

Nicky At least he'll have a chance.

Gary And what about the kids who go to the local shithole like we did?

Nicky They're not my kids.

Gary So fuck them! You reckon they don't feel or think like the brainboxes who pass the exams.

Nicky I didn't say that!

Gary That they won't make enough money to be any use to fucking society.

Nicky I won't apologise for putting my children first.

Gary There's no point in any of it, Nic. Why are you so desperate?

Nicky We can't give them any money and they're not gonna get flats off the council. (*A beat.*) There must be some way to sort this out.

Gary Tell me something. Where can I just be a man? A man, like any other geezer.

Nicky (*a beat*) You should never have gone for the promotion.

Gary You're wrong. I'm glad this happened. I've been burying myself alive Nic. I'd have carried on, pushing the feelings into my blood, poisoning myself. Now she realises who she's dealing with.

Nicky You have to see sense. Because I need you and the kids need you.

Gary I'm gonna set up on my own.

Nicky You tried that once.

Gary That's me done then is it? On the scrap heap?

Nicky Ring up the other firms.

Gary I told you I'm setting up my own business.

Nicky We can't manage without that job. Are you happy living this life? (*Indicates the flat.*) In this place? Five of us in two bedrooms.

Gary Have we ever had rent arrears?

Nicky *half shakes her head.*

Gary Is that fridge ever empty? Name me a time when my kids haven't had new shoes on their feet, leather shoes. Legoland once a year, whatever Nintendo they want at Christmas /

Nicky This isn't about stuff. People are supposed to grow together. To want things together. (*A beat.*) Why did you chase me down at school?

Gary I wanted you. You wanted me an' all. (*A beat.*) Nic, if I go back to work, will you be happy?

Nicky Yeah.

Gary You want me to tolerate Victoria's shit so you can have a bigger kitchen.

Nicky You're making it sound like something else.

Gary After all these years, you don't understand.

Nicky Fucking hell, Gary, how can you say that? Do you remember my dad dragging me home by my hair when he caught us on that bus? Broke two of my ribs after he got me home. He shut the door on me the day I went to show my mum our baby.

Gary At least your dad and his kind said what they felt.

Nicky They talked shit. My dad and yours.

Gary They had their reasons.

Nicky My dad said you weren't capable, that you'd let me down.

Gary Now I have.

Child of the Divide

Sudha Bhuchar

Sudha Bhuchar is an award-winning playwright/actor and founder of Bhuchar Boulevard. As co-founder of Tamasha (with Kristine Landon-Smith), their landmark work includes *A Fine Balance* (adapted from Rohinton Mistry's novel), *Strictly Dandia* and *Fourteen Songs, Two Weddings and a Funeral* (winner Barclays TMA Best Musical). Sudha's solo plays include *Child of the Divide* (Time Out magazine's number 1 family show 2006, winner Asian Media Awards 2018), *The House of Bilquis Bibi* (Lorca's *The House of Bernada Alba* reimagined in contemporary Pakistan) and *My Name Is . . .* (which she adapted for Radio 4 where it was chosen for Pick of the Week).

Writing credits with Shaheen Khan include three series of *Girlies* (Radio 4) and *Balti Kings* for the stage (Tamasha), which they recently transposed to Sydney where it was *The Curry Kings of Parrammatta*. Sudha was writer (with Sapan Saran) on National Theatre of Wales/ Junoon's collaborative exploration of Indian diasporic womanhood in *Sisters*.

Theatre acting credits include Gurpreet Bhatti's *Khandan* (Royal Court and Birmingham Rep), Tanika Gupta's *Lions and Tigers* (Sam Wanamaker Playhouse) and *The Village* by April de Angelis (Theatre Royal Stratford East). TV includes *Coronation Street* (ITV), Ruth Jones's *Stella* (Sky) and *Noughts and Crosses* (BBC). Film credits include Disney's *Mary Poppins Returns*, Ben Wheatley's *Happy New Year Colin Burstead* and Riz Ahmed and Bassam Tariq's upcoming *Mogul Mowgli*. Sudha won a Tongues on Fire Flame award (2018); was a finalist as Best Actress for BBC Radio 4's Audio Drama Awards (2019) for *My Son the Doctor* (co-written with Saleyha Ahsan); and won Eastern Eye's ACTA award for her contribution to the arts (2019).

Sudha is currently working on her evolving one-woman monologue *Evening Conversations* (most recently performed at WOW festival, Southbank) and is under commission to Revolution Arts/Wellcome Collection for *Touchstone Tales*, an exploration of the theme of touch with the communities in Bury Park, Luton through monologues and scenes.

www.bhucharboulevard.com

www.revolutonarts.com/projects/touch-commission

What does the word 'crisis' mean to you in a theatrical sense?

For me 'crisis' in a theatrical sense is when things that have been simmering underneath the surface in the world of the protagonists, like buried secrets, come to the fore and disrupt the situation thus revealing the characters' inner selves and wounds. This inevitably changes them and propels them in a direction they/the audience may not have anticipated.

How do you feel theatre has the ability to represent/respond to global crises?

Theatre can both respond and represent global crises with immediacy, thus enhancing perspectives that appear on the news as 'hard' facts, and reflect deeply on the crises long after they have passed. For me it is the 'lived experience' of people who go through the crises that theatre can capture with great sensitivity and resonance and invite us to examine our own lives in order to live them 'better'.

Why did you pick this specific scene? What is this scene doing at this point of the play?

Pali/Altaaf is the central character in my play *Child of the Divide* and he was born a Hindu but, when he became displaced from his real family, was adopted by a Muslim couple who made him their son Altaaf. Before this scene, we see he has embraced his new identity and family and is comfortable in his skin and new life. Then he is confronted by seeing his old home, which is now occupied by the local bully, Pagal head (literally 'mad head'). Pagal head and his sidekick Buttameez (literally 'ill mannered') beat Pali up when they find out he is a Hindu and in this scene Pali is considering the aftermath of this beating, with his friends Hasina and Aisha. He shares that he hasn't buried his real identity after all and is still longing for his family who lost him. He doesn't realise that his experience will land deeply with Hasina who has a secret of her own – that she is half Hindu/half Muslim – a secret she has never shared before. The other characters Aisha and Buttameez also end up sharing their deepest feelings although the children can't get Buttameez to talk about his deepest wound –that he witnessed the murder of his entire family at the hands of Hindus. The scene is looking at complex questions of identity, blood and belonging through the eyes of children – big subjects that grown-ups can reduce into the binary of 'us' and 'them', which is never the answer.

How does this scene speak beyond the wider context of the play?

This scene invites us to examine our prejudices and biases which is an urgent and explosive conversation today and at the heart of all issues of inequality. Confronting and embracing difference rather than erasing it and examining privilege is the only catalyst for real change. This scene shows how the wisdom of children can pierce through the ignorance of adults who can be entrenched in their tribal thinking.

As a writer, do you feel a point of crisis is always necessary in a play to create/maintain/sustain drama?

I think a point or points of crises are important and necessary, but I don't subscribe to the artificial 'raising of stakes' that writers are too often coached to do where characters become slave to the so-called 'bigger story' and become unbelievable. Crises can creep up slowly and cumulatively without necessarily resulting in scenes of 'high drama'. This can be more powerful to watch than a lot of shouting and violence on stage. A friend and peer Carl Miller described my recent work as 'epic in miniature' which I felt was the highest compliment.

Does theatre as a form allow for a more effective exploration of crisis in terms of what can be explored, presented and communicated to an audience, in relation to other creative forms?

I think all art forms can explore crisis effectively but the uniqueness of theatre is that it is a 'shared' experience with the audience and that gives it a magic and spark that can't be replicated in other creative forms. It also allows for people to reflect and carry on talking together after the curtain has fallen in a way that other art forms are more 'solitary' in how they are experienced.

When constructing a play how do you effectively boil down larger global themes that could otherwise be overwhelming for characters within 'their world' so that they can find room to resonate?

When exploring large global themes, like the partition of India in *Child of the Divide*, my approach is always to look at the lives of ordinary people who find themselves in extraordinary situations. So, to ask from their point of view, how would they experience these big global events in their everyday lives? So, the children in *Child of the Divide* experience trauma and displacement and yet never find the 'line' that their parents told them was 'drawn' dividing India and Pakistan. In another of my plays, *My*

Name Is . . . the bigger debates of 'Islam vs the West' propagated in the media are distilled through a 'tug of love' true story of a half-Pakistani/half-white Scottish girl who runs away from home leaving both parents fighting for her custody.

What do you feel is the biggest threat to the creation of new drama and plays given the current global crisis? Do we need theatre now more than ever?

I feel the biggest threat to the creation of new drama is the uncertainty around when we will be able to/have the confidence to 'congregate' together again in the same physical space and sharing the same experience. There is also a lot of uncertainty around the survival of theatre buildings and spaces and I hope that will be resolved. It's great to see the innovation and activity in the creation of new work digitally and reaching online audiences but, in my mind, this can't irrevocably replace the 'magic' of live theatre for live audiences. Yes, we 'need' theatre now more than ever, judging by the appetite for online archive shows. I have been working on a Wellcome Collection/Revoluton Arts new co-commission exploring the theme of 'touch' with communities in Luton and have had to reframe the exploration in terms of 'absence of touch'. The response to the engagement work and monologues *Touchstone Tales* from online audiences has shown me the power of stories resonating at this moment of time when people are in isolation and feel 'listened' to.

As a child growing up in Tanzania, India, Norfolk and London, my family went through so much displacement and turbulent times. I never imagined that these experiences and crises would be a storehouse of memories to draw from that would enable me to explore the stories of my communities and carve a career within theatre. Although 'uncertainty' has been the only 'certainty' in my life, I hope that we will come through this crisis stronger and be able to come together through theatre.

***Child of the Divide* premiered at the Polka Theatre, London in 2006 and its future life to date includes Webplay/Tamasha's tour to LA/ New York (2007), Bhuchar Boulevard's remount to mark the seventieth anniversary of the partition of India (2017) and Junior Festival at Harbourfront Centre, Toronto (2018). The 2017 republished text includes forewords by historian Professor Sarah Ansari from Royal Holloway University and Iqbal Singh from The National Archives, contextualising the play within the history of the period.**

Summer 1947. Sixteen million people are on the move between India and the newly formed Pakistan. Amid the violent political upheaval, young Pali's fingers slip from his father's hand, and his destiny changes for ever. Lost, dispossessed and alone, Pali is saved by a Muslim family. The boy is given a new name, a new faith and a new life and family. Seven years later when his real father returns to claim him, Pali's life is turned upside down again. He is forced to decide who he is: the Hindu boy he was born to be, the Muslim boy he has become or simply a child of the divide.

Inspired by Bhisham Sahni's short story 'Pali', this is a story of family, identity and belonging. It is set against a fractured landscape of displacement, families torn apart and stolen pasts; where friendship and love are found in unexpected places.

Scene Nine

A little while later. **Pali** *is with* **Aisha** *and* **Hasina**.

Pali *comforts himself with his quilt.* **Hasina** *wipes his bruises.*

Hasina I didn't know you was Hindu.

Aisha He's not. Maulvi Sahib made him Muslim

Pali Pitaji said people are people but he lied.

Hasina Some people are just bad.

Aisha Like that Pagal head.

Hasina And Buttameez. I thought he was our friend.

Aisha We'll get them.

Pali They're bigger than us.

Aisha We'll tell Maulvi Sahib and your ammi and abu.

Pali They're not my mum and dad. My real mum and dad lost me.

Hasina Maybe they're looking for you.

Pali I wish I was a baby then they could have carried me like they did Gudiya.

Hasina Why don't you think about them? If you think about someone really really hard, then they think about you at the same time.

Aisha That's stupid.

Hasina It's true. My ammi said.

Pali I'm scared, I'll forget my mataji.

Burying his head in his quilt.

But I remember her smell.

Hasina I think about my ammi all the time and I know she thinks about me.

Aisha So why doesn't she come and get you?

Hasina She thinks I'm safe with my uncle.

Pali So why are you in the refugee camp?

Hasina Can I tell you a secret?

Aisha Not another secret? My heart's gonna burst.

Pali Allah ki kasam, We won't tell.

Hasina I'm half–half so I got two names. Hasina cos my abu said I was his beautiful princess and Sita which was my secret with my mama.

Pali Sita? Hindu name like Pali?

Aisha Lord Ram's wife. We studied it at school. Before all the Hindus left. Now we're not supposed to know. She was kidnapped by that Raavan, isn't it?

Hasina Sita stayed pure but like no one believed her and, in the end, she asked Mother Earth to take her back.

Pali I thought Ram and Sita had a happy ending.

Hasina Mama said Sita was too good for this world. But I'm bad. My uncle said that my abu died because of me.

Pali S'not true.

Hasina Hindus killed him cos he married a Hindu and they don't like that. Bloods shouldn't mix. But mine is.

Pali If you cut do you bleed different colours?

Aisha Don't be stupid.

Hasina Because of my Muslim blood, My mama sent me with my uncle to be safe here in Pakistan. Because of my Hindu blood, my uncle left me by the side of the road. Sitting on a stone . . . alone. He said he couldn't love me because in my face he could see the Hindus that killed his brother. I loved my abba . . . Allah ki kasam . . . He made me pretty things and (*looking at her battered shoes*) decorated my shoes with tarey and sequins. A soft lady found me. She took my hand and brought me to the camp across the border. I came with other lost children like Buttameez.

Pali I never knew that.

Hasina You're lucky your new mum loves you. She's always calling you in to eat a sweet rusk or khatai.

Pali It's like she doesn't want me to be hungry. But sometimes her treats stick in my throat and I'm still hungry. I think about my real mum and dad. Why did they lose me?

Aisha Wish I could take my ammi to the mum swap shop.

Hasina You don't mean it.

Aisha I do. I always have to hug and kiss her to cheer her up. It frightens me. When she's angry, I'm calm; when she's upset, I'm cheerful; when she's silly, I'm silly. She plays tickle monster and we laugh and laugh till we cry. Then she can't stop. She even cries on my birthday and Eid. When she's sad, I hate her.

Hasina My amma will come and get me.

Pali How do you know?

Hasina I post her a letter every day.

Buttameez *approaches the trio tentatively.*

Pali Thought you was my friend.

Buttameez You didn't tell me you was Hindu.

Aisha And you didn't tell us you was evil?

Buttameez Don't you know Hindus hate us?

Hasina Who says?

Buttameez (*to* **Pali**, *not really hearing* **Hasina**) I wanna know why you hate us.

Pali I hate you cos you hit me.

Buttameez I hit you cos you hate me.

Pali I don't.

Buttameez You do. You Hindus told us to leave India.

Pali And you Muslims told us to leave Pakistan.

Buttameez I didn't. I wasn't even here.

Pali And I didn't. I wasn't even there.

Buttameez I didn't want to leave.

Pali Nor did I but I wish I had now.

Buttameez I just wanted to play bante with my friends.

Pali Me too.

Buttameez But they looked at me,

And turned away.

Their eyes

Pure enemy.

Pali I didn't turn away from you. You hit me.

Aisha Just cos that Pagal head told you to.

Hasina You should think for yourself, not just follow bullies.

Buttameez (*meaning* **Pali**) He made me mental. Never seen a Hindu since we walked all the way here from India to get away from them.

Hasina Yes you have.

Buttameez Haven't.

Hasina You've seen me.

Buttameez You're not one of them.

Hasina Half of me is them.

Buttameez Why didn't you say?

Hasina Didn't want your hate like my uncle's

Buttameez Why should I hate you?

Hasina You'd look at my face and see the Hindus that killed your family.

Buttameez You're my best friend. Only one from my desh.

Hasina And Pali . . . Altaaf is my friend.

It sinks in to **Buttameez**.

Buttameez (*to* **Pali**) Sorry, dude.

Pali Yeah. Me too.

Aisha What happened to your family?

Buttameez Nothing.

Pali If you don't tell, you might forget.

Buttameez I want to forget but it won't let me.

Aisha Tell us then.

Buttameez No!

Hasina Leave him.

Pali Come on, let's play tag. Bhago, I'm it.

He hops on one leg and chases the others exuberantly.

Glossary

abu/abba	father (term used by Muslims)
Allah ki kasam	I swear by Allah
ammi/amma	mother (term used by Muslims)
bante	marbles
desh	country/homeland
khatai/khatais	a type of biscuit/biscuits
mataji	mother (term used by Hindus)
tarey	stars

Jess and Joe Forever

Zoe Cooper

Zoe Cooper is a playwright and theatre practitioner. Her latest play *Out of Water* ran at the Orange Tree Theatre in spring 2019, produced in association with the RSC, and was a finalist in the 2020 Susan Smith Blackburn Prize. It was also shortlisted for the Charles Wintour Award for Most Promising Playwright at the Evening Standard Awards 2019, and nominated for the Best New Production of a Play Award in the Broadway World UK Awards.

Her play *Jess and Joe Forever* won her the Most Promising Playwright Award at the Off West End Awards 2017 and was longlisted for the Evening Standard Most Promising Playwright Award for its production at the Orange Tree. It then went on a UK tour, played at the Traverse Theatre during the Edinburgh Festival 2017 and was revived at the Stephen Joseph Theatre in October 2018. It has since enjoyed productions in Australia and the Czech Republic, and is forthcoming in the USA.

What does the word 'crisis' mean to you in a theatrical sense?

I think some of the best drama is created when characters come to understand that they are being prevented from getting what they want or from keeping it – and choose to act. In *The Seagull* by Anton Chekhov Nina undertakes all sorts of actions in order to be noticed by an inconsistently attentive Boris; to become an actress; to break free and stay free. In *Top Girls* by Caryl Churchill, Marlene has come to understand that she has to choose between having a family life and being a successful career woman in eighties Thatcherite Britain and acts accordingly in a number of complex ways throughout the play. In *random* by debbie tucker green, a family comes to terms with the loss of a member; through telling their story they understand the reasons why they lost him and how their pain is being silenced. In these plays there is not necessarily a single moment of crisis, but the characters are increasingly in crisis and act accordingly.

How do you feel theatre has the ability to represent or respond to global crises?

We in theatre have a vital role in representing our world. Our world is in crisis in this moment, but then again it has been in crisis in various ways since time began. The manner in which writers respond will depend on the kind of writers they already are. Some will want to write very directly and quickly, almost journalistically, to represent the current circumstances urgently. Others might wait for years to respond, and/or when they do it might be tangentially. *London Road* by Alecky Blythe was a musical that explored the ways a contemporary community reacted to a series of murders of sex workers in Suffolk using that community's verbatim words; *The Welkin* by Lucy Kirkwood was about a woman accused of murder in the eighteenth century and how the possibility of her being pregnant might have helped her escape hanging. These plays were created using different methods and represent, respond to and refract their subject in different ways. But both plays tell us something about the moral codes around women's behaviour and crime through the centuries and in the present moment.

What is this scene doing at this point of the play?

Up to this point in the play Joe has invited the audience to see him as he sees himself: a working-class lad from a rural community with a mother who sadly died in childbirth. But in this moment Joe is forced to reconcile this self with the way that the other people in the community, and even members of his own family, sometimes see him: a child assigned female at birth, who they still think of as a girl.

How does this scene speak beyond the wider context of the play?

In writing *Jess and Joe Forever* I wanted to create a romantic comedy in which a trans-male character had a happy ending. At the time of writing, stories about trans-men were very often mired in violence against the trans-male body, for example in the film *Boys Don't Cry* where the protagonist was shot to death and then beaten. The film was based on the real life murder of Brandon Teena, and I don't deny that showing the reality of the harm done to queer bodies in a heteronormative society is vital work. But in writing my play some years later I wanted to offer an alternative reality, one where a trans-boy might encounter real prejudice and difficulty but where ultimately his story would conclude with a big Hollywood kiss. This scene is part of telling that story.

As a writer, do you feel a point of crisis is always necessary in a play to create, maintain or sustain drama?

Many of my favourite plays don't seem to have one. *Circle, Mirror, Transformation* by Annie Baker, *Kitchen Sink* by Tom Wells, *Sweat* by Lynn Nottage, *Being Friends* by Robert Holman. I don't think any of these have a single moment where everything comes to a head. There are lots of little moments of sublimated, diffused or growing crisis. In my experience that is often how life operates. Maybe that is why I love these plays.

Does theatre as a form allow for a more effective exploration of crisis in terms of what can be explored, presented and communicated to an audience, in relation to other creative forms?

Well, I suppose form dictates meaning. So Picasso's explosive painting of *Guernica*, in black and white, populated with somewhat abstract people and animals, offers us a snapshot of a specific event in the Spanish Civil War, and in so doing illuminates something broader about the chaos and violence of the machine of war. In the novel *The Prime of Miss Jean Brodie* by Muriel Spark, a young school girl leaves Edinburgh to fight in the Spanish Civil War at the urging of her enigmatic teacher; later in the novel we learn that she was killed before she even got there. In this way we are being invited to understand something about the possibility of the multiple motivations of the individual young men and women caught up in conflicts. This is achieved through the broader temporal scope of the novel and because novels often allow us to see inside the heads of characters. I suppose in theatre there are almost always bodies on stage, they almost always speak to each other, and it is through these relationships that we come to understand something about ourselves and the society we live in.

When constructing a play how do you effectively boil down larger global themes that could otherwise be overwhelming for characters within 'their world' so that they can find room to resonate?

For me the impetus to write comes from a niggling annoyance that sometimes grows into a rage that a particular story is not being told. I wrestle with this feeling for a year or more as I develop the world of the play, the characters and the plot. I try not to dwell too much on the 'larger global themes' a play might contain because I find that this overburdens it, weighing it down with portentous 'meaning'. I just want to tell the story that I think is missing, that I think needs to be told.

What do you feel is the biggest threat to the creation of new drama and plays given the current global crisis? Do we need theatre now more than ever?

I think the biggest threat is that, in the face of economic downturn that will follow the pandemic, we revert to 'safe' programming of theatre.

Safe programming normally means programming plays by white, straight, dead men. There are some brilliant white straight dead male writers, but our theatre is more interesting because it is diverse, weird and challenging. I hope that the younger generation of black female writers in particular (Temi Wilkey, Yasmin Joseph and Jasmine Lee-Jones amongst others) continue to be commissioned, produced, published. We need them.

I am also very worried about how our regional theatres will survive and continue thrive. I live in Newcastle, which is also where my first play was produced, We have three theatres in Newcastle: Northern Stage, Live Theatre and Alphabetti. Northern Stage produces big-scale ambitious theatre and heart-filled inclusive Christmas shows, Live Theatre is one of the only theatres dedicated solely to new writing outside of London. Alphabetti is an award-winning new fringe theatre. I am crossing my fingers that in our already economically scarred but wonderfully creative city we can continue to make work together.

***Jess and Joe Forever* premiered at the Orange Tree Theatre, London in September 2016**

Meet Jess and Joe. They want to tell you their story. Joe is Norfolk born and bred and wears wellies. Jess holidays there with her au pair and is slightly too tubby for her summer dresses. They are miles apart even when they stand next to each other. This is a story of growing up, fitting in (or not), boys, girls, secrets, Scotch eggs and maybe even love, but most of all it's about friendship.

Spanning several summer holidays, *Jess and Joe Forever* is an unusual coming-of-age tale that explores rural life and what it means to belong somewhere, if you can really belong anywhere.

Thirteen

As **Joe** *speaks* **Jess** *binds his chest. As he continues this action gets faster and covers more of his torso.*

Joe In February at the Unit we are doing about the Egyptians and we are doing about mummies and how the ancient Egyptians would not bury their bodies in wet ground but instead would preserve them (because Egypt is a hot country) at first in hot pits that would naturally preserve all their skin and their organs and that and then because of religion how they started to believe that preservation was really important for having a good afterlife and that is why they then would have themselves preserved on purpose with what is called embalming and they would be put in tombs with things that showed what they did in life, which would be gold jewellery or pots or things like that. And at the Unit because a lot of the girls struggle with what is called 'traditional learning methods' we do a lot of fun stuff that is not just reading. So today the girls are wrapping me up in bandages. Like a mummy. And I quite like the feeling of their hands wrapping me up and I am thinking that it is a shame, it is a shame that my mum was burnt and that she was not mummified instead. And I wonder what she looked like (because I only have a few blurred photographs because this was before Facebook) and I think about that phone call that I overheard which was Dad on the phone to Aunty Irene and saying that I was the spit of her. 'Joe is the absolute spit of her now . . . she is the spit of her and perhaps I have made a mistake, Reeny, because she doesn't, because she has stopped playing with the other boys from the village and now she's in that Unit and she just seems so . . . so . . . so maybe I should have, maybe it would have been kinder to make her, make her be a girl, to stop all this nonsense of letting her pretend to be a boy and make her be a girl, because she has started to develop and they can all, everyone can see now.' And I start to panic in the bandages.

Joe *starts to struggle against the binding and* **Jess** *starts to pull at the loops.*

Joe And I have to be unravelled and have a little sit down in the Quiet Area and this is when the teacher tells me about the god, the Egyptian god with the dog's head and how he could make things change.

Jess *is pulling at the loops hard, down round* **Joe***'s hips and* **Joe** *collapses on the floor.*

Joe How if you prayed to him he could make things transform if he thought that was a good idea and that is when I realise that this is what must have happened in the bathroom in our house next to the avocado three-piece as my mum was on all fours panting and wanting and willing me to come out. Praying for me to come out.

Joe *is finally kicking free.* **Jess** *and* **Joe** *lie exhausted on the floor.*

Joe Because even though I was born wrong she knew, she could see I was a boy even if I didn't look like one, she knew, she knew before she died, in her heart she could see, I was a boy, not a girl, a boy – Joseph, her Joseph.

Joe *stands up*

After that we do hieroglyphics which is Egyptian picture writing.

The King of Hell's Palace

Frances Ya-Chu Cowhig

Frances Ya-Chu Cowhig is an internationally produced playwright whose work has been staged in the United Kingdom by the Royal Shakespeare Company, the National Theatre, Hampstead Theatre, Trafalgar Studios 2 and the Unicorn Theatre. In the United States her work has been staged at venues that include the Oregon Shakespeare Festival, Manhattan Theater Club and the Goodman Theatre. Frances's plays have been awarded the Wasserstein Prize, the Yale Drama Series Award (selected by David Hare), an Edinburgh Fringe First Award, the David A. Callichio Award and the Keene Prize for Literature. Her work has been published by Yale University Press, Glimmer Train, Methuen Drama, Samuel French and Dramatists Play Service. Frances was born in Philadelphia, and raised in Northern Virginia, Okinawa, Taipei and Beijing. She received an MFA in Writing from the James A. Michener Center for Writers at UT Austin, a BA in Sociology from Brown University and a certificate in Ensemble-Based Physical Theatre from the Dell'Arte International School of Physical Theatre.

What does the word 'crisis' mean to you in a theatrical sense?

That one or more characters has been confronted with a new reality, truth or system of meaning. A choice must be made – and, of course, wilful ignorance is also a choice.

As a writer, do you feel a point of crisis is always necessary in a play to create/maintain/sustain drama?

Absolutely, but it could be a tiny domestic crisis between two people, or an inner crisis of faith that only one person is having. A crisis is a catalyst for the play, and no matter whether it is intimate or epic, it should have consequences for the world of the play and its characters.

Does theatre as a form allow for more effective exploration of crisis in terms of what can be explored, presented and communicated to an audience, in relation to other creative forms?

To me, what is ideal about theatre as a form is that there is no definitive version of a play – it is designed to be produced again and again by different groups of people with different production capacities. A group of teenagers putting on a play in a garage with props they find around the house can create a performance experience more potent and immediate than a version of the play that cost millions of dollars to stage on Broadway or the West End. It is that scalability that excites me about theatre – the text of a stage play is simply a plan for a live experience.

When constructing a play how do you effectively boil down larger global themes that could otherwise be overwhelming for characters within 'their world' so that they can find room to resonate?

I try to find a way to make the global theme a metaphor that I can embed into the plot structure. I look for storylines that can resonate on a metaphorical level. In *The King of Hell's Palace*, the Chinese government is literally profiting from the blood of farmers and killing them by spreading HIV infection. This is a real life story inspired by the life and activism of Chinese public health official and whistleblower Dr Wang Shuping. Shuping, who passed away a week after the play premiered at Hampstead Theatre in London in 2019, was a beloved family friend, and very generous with providing insight into the personalities of the public health officials she worked with during the Henan AIDS crisis. She also shared a lot of specific details about how her work as a whistleblower caused the deterioration and dissolution of her first marriage. These recollections helped me develop the storylines in ways that could also be relatable to the audience. I chose to ground both storylines (rural and urban) in the tradition of the family drama. One storyline became about the rural villagers who were trying to pull themselves out of poverty by selling their blood, and the other about the married public health officials responsible for running the blood stations. Telling the story through intimate family relationships helped me distil the global themes in the play into specific personal stories.

What do you feel is the biggest threat to the creation of new drama and plays given the current global crisis? Do we need theatre now more than ever?

What we need now more than ever is earnest, sincere people with strong moral compasses going into politics and holding positions of power. We need a life working in a government and public office to not be seen as the domain of the cynical or the corrupt. Funneling our brightest and most charismatic young people into a life solely in the arts is not a net good for a society. If anything, it is an effective way for a ruling elite to maintain social control.

We need to stop making being an 'artist' a professional path, and instead find ways to nurture the artistic sides of all people, so that there can be more original plays written and produced on the community level, by people who are also teachers and social workers and janitors. Instead of theatre being produced in a few cities and then 'trickling down' to smaller towns and rural areas, I dream of a world in which everyone has time to make art and grow in their artistry and share it with others in their community – and perhaps some of that production will travel and be seen in larger cities, but it should be decentralised and grounded in community.

This is also the kind of theatre that is not ecologically catastrophic because, let's be honest, people flying around the world to see plays and rehearse plays (and I include myself in this indictment) are doing far more harm ecologically than good.

How do you feel theatre has the ability to represent/respond to global crises?

What is most potent about the form of theatre is that it requires people to breathe together and experience a story together in a shared physical space for a specific duration of time. The Covid-19 pandemic has shown many of us how precious and rare that can be in a time where more and more life is lived on and through screens.

There are plays that reinforce the values of the ruling elite and act as potent forms of social control, and there are plays that attempt to dream us into a more equitable, sustainable future. Theatre can hold all kinds of stories, and represent an incredibly wide range of worlds and views – but its ability to represent or respond to any crisis depends on what types of stories producers are willing to support, how those shows get marketed, and what kind of audiences are engaged through the work, and how conversations around the themes and ideas of the play are curated and amplified.

Why did you pick this specific scene? What is this scene doing at this point of the play?

The King of Hell's Palace opens in 1992, when China is beginning to lay the foundations for global wealth and power. In the populous province of Henan, a rural family has been recruited into a new and unusual trade that promises to pull them out of poverty – selling their blood to the government. But amidst the hype and the soaring profits, an infectious disease specialist at the Ministry of Health realises that, due to official corruption and cost-cutting measures, the blood plasma collection stations are contaminated, and becoming vectors for the spread of HIV.

This scene is the final scene of the play. It occurs six years after the rural family the play follows has began selling their blood to the Henan government. All but one member of the family has become infected with AIDS. The family has tried to appeal to the government for help, only to be met with brutal police force, and told that all matters related to the question of AIDS in Henan Province have been classified a state secret.

Earlier in the play the rural family has heard of peasants throwing themselves in front of gravel trucks on the highway, so that the family of the dead can sue the gravel company for compensation. Left with no other choice, and desperate to find a way to secure AIDS medication once it enters the country, two adult brothers, Wen and Kuan, decide to take matters into their own hands.

***The King of Hell's Palace* originally ran at London's Hampstead Theatre in September 2019**

When the Henan Ministry of Health begins paying citizens for blood plasma which is then sold to pharmaceutical companies, impoverished farmers in the province's remote villages sell blood to buy fertiliser, mend their houses and create a better life for their children. As corrupt health officials cut costs to maximise profits, safety standards are ignored, bringing potential catastrophe to China's most vulnerable population.

Inspired by the real life story of Chinese public health official and whistleblower Dr Wang Shuping, this gripping drama explores the conflicts that arise when a community's greatest source of capital becomes their own bodies. Focusing on the personal repercussions of the cover-up, *The King of Hell's Palace* questions how political and medical decisions are made and how both a family and an entire country can look to recover from traumatic events.

Scene Twelve

1998. Henan, China. Rural highway. Night. **Wen**, *a peasant, and* **Kuan**, *his older brother, walk along the shoulder, carrying flashlights and smoking cigarettes. The sound of frogs, crickets, night birds, passing cars and wind blowing through trees.*

Kuan Don't forget to fertilize the peony fields next week. Use compost, crushed bones and rotted manure.

Wen I'm not good with living things.

Kuan You overdo it. They're carefree flowers. They do better with less attention.

Wen Remember how quiet it was during the famine?

Kuan (–)

Wen No birds. No bugs. No leaves to be blown by the wind. Back then I thought hell was a place without sound.

He listens to the night.

It's going to be quiet like that again.

Kuan When it's winter, don't smother them with mulch. If it's cold, cover our girls lightly with shredded bark or pine needles.

Wen Pei-Pei put one parent in the ground already.

Kuan You sold blood for my daughter. It's right I repay my debts to your family.

Wen That's idiot math.

Kuan If ants swarm the buds, don't spray them. They kill bud-eating pests, and don't hurt the plant.

A truck approaches. **Kuan** *puts out his cigarette.* **Wen** *stiffens.*

Wen Brother –

Kuan When fall comes, cut their stems down, level with the soil and –

Wen Let me do it.

Kuan Compost the blossoms and petals.

Wen Little Yi has two parents.

Kuan When you get medicine, save it all for Little Yi. It's better to help one person live a long time than give everyone a few months.

The sound of the truck approaching. A bright light appears in the distance.

Wen He's stubborn. He won't take more than his share.

Kuan Put something else in your pill bottles. Take it when he gets the real thing.

Wen Wait. Brother –

Kuan *turns off his flashlight. He motions for* **Wen** *to do the same.*

Kuan I'll call out the license plate. Don't settle for less than ninety thousand.

He steps onto the highway – then is yanked back, as **Wen** *lunges forward and pulls him to safety. The sound of the truck passing. Headlights fade. The brothers fight.*

Wen I'd rather die a death of a thousand cuts than outlive my wife. I thought I could face it but I can't. She wants me to be the strong one, but I can't be. I can't watch her die. Please don't make me shame myself. Let me be a hero. If you go, I'll wait for the next truck and follow you out of this world.

Let her remember me as the man who fought for his family until his last breath. Alive I'm worth nothing. Let my death buy my son medicine. Let my flesh feed our flowers. Some people have meaningful lives. Let my death have a meaning. Please, brother. Give this to me.

Kuan *steps aside.* **Wen** *stands on the edge of the highway and faces the approaching truck. He tries to step onto the road. His knees buckle. His body's frozen in fear. He pounds on his legs with his fists.*

Wen MOVE!

Kuan You have life in you still. This isn't your end.

He steps into the blinding headlights of an oncoming truck.

Loud, long honk.

In the next life we'll be a family again.

The whoosh of blood rushing through arteries, increasing to a deafening oceanic volume as –

Pei-Pei, **Kuan***'s daughter, pushes an oversize altar onstage. The altar contains framed portraits of* **Old Yang**, **Wen**, **Kuan**, **Lili**, **Luo Na** *and* **Han-Han** *– family members who have died from AIDS they contracted by selling their blood to the government – and is decorated with offerings for the dead – paper joss clothing, food, incense, beer and peonies.*

Little Yi, **Wen***'s son, approaches, supported by a cane. His clothes hang off his body. Though pale and weak, he still has his familiar swagger. He lights a handful of incense, then hands half to* **Pei-Pei**.

Ocean sounds subside as **Little Yi** *and* **Pei-Pei** *kneel in front of the altar, and bow three times. The ghosts of* **Old Yang**, **Wen**, **Kuan**, **Lili**, **Luo Na** *and* **Han-Han** *enter. They might approach the altar, surrounding the living, or they might appear on a different level, in another realm.*

Ghosts (*singing*)
High above on the mountain side
Floats a cloud so white
There lies peaceful Kangding town
Bathed in silver moonlight
Moonlight shines bright
Over Kangding Town oh . . .

End of play.

Adler & Gibb

Tim Crouch

Tim Crouch is a critically acclaimed and award-winning playwright, director and performer. His plays include *My Arm* (Traverse Theatre/tour), *An Oak Tree* (Traverse Theatre, National Theatre, Off-Broadway/tour), *ENGLAND – a play for galleries* (Traverse Theatre/Fruitmarket Gallery/ Whitechapel Gallery/tour), *The Author* (Royal Court Theatre/tour), *I, Malvolio, I, Peaseblossom, I, Banquo, I, Caliban* (Brighton Festival/tour), what happens to the hope at the end of the evening (with Andy Smith – Almeida festival/tour), *Adler & Gibb* (Royal Court/tour), *Beginners* (Unicorn Theatre), *Total Immediate Collective Imminent Terrestrial Salvation* (NTS/Royal Court/tour), *I, Cinna* (the poet) (RSC, Unicorn Theatre). Directing credits include *The Complete Deaths for Spymonkey*, *Jeramee*, *Hartleby* and *Oooglemore* (Unicorn Theatre/tour), *PEAT* (The Ark, Dublin) and *Antony and Cleopatra* (Gate Theatre, London). He created and co-wrote the BBC TV series *Don't Forget the Driver* which won Best Comedy at the Venice TV Festival, 2019.

Other awards include an OBIE Special Citation, Writers Guild of Great Britain – Best Play for Young Audiences, Prix Italia for Best Radio Adaptation, two Total Theatre Awards, a Fringe First, Herald Angel and Archangel, and the John Whiting Award which he shared with Lucy Kirkwood in 2010.

What does the word 'crisis' mean to you in a theatrical sense?

Crisis is a point of juncture, a crossroads. A moment where things can no longer stay the same; where something has to give, change or break.

In terms of dramatic structure, I suppose every play should have this moment – even if the change that's needed doesn't come (e.g. *Godot*). Crisis is the bedrock of the fabled 'conflict' we talk about when we talk about drama. Crisis is the trigger to dramatic action.

The definition of crisis also applies to theatre in general. UK theatre itself is currently the protagonist in a conflict where I feel things can no longer stay the same, where something has to give. In many ways, the pandemic of 2020 has exposed that state of crisis and given us the distance to see it more clearly. Long before Covid-19, UK theatre had mostly become the exclusionary domain of the well-off, the privileged and the powerful – specialised, packaged and priced beyond the access of underrepresented voices. It's been removed from schools and curriculums, defunded out of communities and youth provision. Productions are increasingly underwritten by the capital value of celebrity actors, gimmicks, tie-ins to other forms (books, films, music). The crisis of theatre is that it's become a capitalistic art form and the pandemic has exposed capitalism as ultimately having no solutions to our human condition. For a culture that professes inclusion, theatre seems to be compounding the segregation that it rails against. The imbalances are glaring. Something has to change.

How do you feel theatre has the ability to represent/respond to global crises?

Theatre is not a toolbox for social transformation or a remedy for social ill. It's not even that much of an accurate bellwether to the future. If theatre is to avoid being an adjunct to journalism, then it must be allowed to be itself: discursive, digressive, tangential, impulsive, metaphorical, lyrical, uncertain. The core values of theatre are not its campaigning strengths. I think theatre sees crisis as a constant ongoing process in life. Theatre's primary ability at any time is to help us to gather together and see laterally; to momentarily give some form to formlessness; to perceive the imperceptible; to conceive the inconceivable.

Why did you pick this specific scene? What is this scene doing at this point of the play?

This scene is when the formal muscle of *Adler & Gibb* starts to flex and evolve. Until this moment in the play, all action on stage has been abstract: two actors facing out and an invitation to the audience to 'see' the action of the story without it being shown. I used to say that *Adler & Gibb* slowly shoots itself in the foot. The first third is, for me, the more interesting – its dissonance between what the eye sees and what the mind sees. Then, gradually, the play becomes increasingly figurative until, at the end, the form breaks through into film. In the film, the things we saw with our mind's eye at the start of the play are finally shown in photo-reality – the house, the Winnebago, the dog, the deer, the gun, the angle grinder, etc. The play charts a journey of attenuation to the imaginative process – both formally and narratively. At the beginning, it operates on a more imaginative and collaborative level with the audience than it does at the end. I think I'm saying, 'Look how much more fun this is! To be included, to be needed, to resolve the contradictions. Let's enjoy the game that realism can exclude us from.' And then I slowly close the game down – in the way that I perceive that game to be closed down on wider cultural and social levels.

The form of the play is straining towards imitation – just as the character of Louise is straining towards authentic imitation in the role she will play in the biopic of Adler's life. At the start of this scene, Louise has been upstairs in Gibb's house, raiding the belongings of the late Janet Adler. She presents herself to Gibb, dressed as Adler, and Gibb is momentarily taken in. That act of appropriation deepens with Louise's 'perfect impersonation' of Adler's voice – and then, finally, Louise 'walks' as Adler. The stage direction: '*This is the first time the fictional space is broken with a completed action.*' Louise 'becomes' Adler as an actor is trained to 'become' another, as Daniel Day-Lewis becomes Lincoln, or Meryl Streep becomes Thatcher, or Rami Malek becomes Freddie Mercury, or Salma Hayek becomes Frida Kahlo and so on. The person who was Janet Adler becomes 'owned' by Louise:

When that movie is released, whether you help us or not, I will become your lover. To all the world, I will *become* her. I won't only be the actress who played her, I will *be* her. Be her. The real Janet is a long-time dead and buried in the yard now, that's distant history now. When they think of Janet Adler, they will think of me.

I place this striving for an owned reality against the playful non-proprietorial freedom of abstraction. That freedom is given to the children in *Adler & Gibb* and a connection is made between abstraction and play. The children represent 'deer' without having to own deer, represent dog without having to get on all fours. They give the idea of these things to the audience to play with. In this scene, the character of Louise destroys that sense of play as she is driven by those capitalistic impulses to succeed. The killing of the dog in *Adler & Gibb* is like the death of play – but done playfully. We understand that the child represents dog. We understand that the pool noodle swim float represents the shovel we saw at the beginning of the scene. When the actor harmlessly (playfully) thwacks the child with the foam float, we understand that Louise Mane is savagely hacking the dog to death. The dog is the 'art dog' that Adler and Gibb offered to the Whitney's permanent collection. The dog – beloved companion of Margaret Gibb. The dog who sniffs out the fake of Louise Mane. The dog who sat by Adler's grave for weeks. Boy. 'Look how old he's gotten.'

The killing of the dog in *Adler & Gibb* feels like a defining gesture in my work. In the play of mine prior to this one, *The Author*, I challenge hyper-naturalistic representations of violence in art and theatre. I remember saying in conversations around *The Author* that there are better ways to represent violence that working hard to make it look real. Art's job is not to slavishly imitate but to generate the sense of one thing in something else. The killing of the dog is my offer to that argument. It's a shocking moment – felt viscerally by the audience who understand what it means. We see the violence of it, the significance of it, without having to be shown an attempt at its reality.

Not long after this moment, at the Royal Court Theatre, a real dog was brought on stage and presented by its owner – a different dog and owner at each performance. There are multiple versions of the dog in *Adler & Gibb*: the dog in our heads, the child as dog, the real dog on the stage – and then the 'real' dog in the film at the end.

As Sam says later in the play, Louise kills the art:

Louise I killed the fucking art-dog!

Sam You killed the art!

Vincent van Dog.

Louise Jackson Poodle. Pug-casso.

Sam Husky Warhol.

How does this scene speak beyond the wider context of the play?

I think I set out to write about the fetishisation and commercialisation of reality – both in the media and in the world. Sam's dying speech towards the end of *Adler & Gibb* parallels the language of a Hollywood acting coach with right-wing motivational speakers: how you must overcome your obstacle and get what you want. The US acting coach Ivana Chubbuck summed it up for me: 'I teach actors how to win because this is what people do in real life! They go after what they want. Interesting and dynamic people go after what they want in interesting and dynamic ways, creating greater emotion and intensity in realizing these goals . . . Use your pain and win your goals.' I find this position nauseating – and antithetical to both art and humanity. I see manifestations of this attitude everywhere: the correlation between pain and success, winning and losing, trampling over anything to get what you want.

I also think that we're in a crisis of representation – of how we show and see ourselves. I live in hope that this crisis is the crossroads that will facilitate a change. My work is mostly inspired by a need to challenge the dominant realist modes of theatre: that fully rendered, figurative 'otherness' achieved through psychologically driven virtuoso performance; through set, props, costume, money spent. This obsession with materiality leaves theatre lingering in some half-light between film and television. Theatre's unique liveness is often sacrificed in the name of fixing the transformation before the audience have even arrived.

There is also a question in my work about the dominance of materiality in the world. The model of artist presented by Janet Adler and Margaret Gibb is anti-capitalist and anti-material – to the point where they never actually existed . . . They rejected the commodification of their work. Their 1998 manifesto was named 'there are now enough objects' – and I suppose I side with this statement on many terms, not least in theatre. I'm excited by how little we need to achieve what we want. Adler and Gibb's work came from their love for one another and from the limitless possibilities of thought, not things.

Does theatre as a form allow for a more effective exploration of crisis in terms of what can be explored, presented and communicated to an audience, in relation to other creative forms?

Theatre enables us to posit something in time and space. To propose a possibility, a model, a hypothesis of living and thinking and being and structuring thought – which can then be worked through at a distance, scrutinised, empathised, inhabited, entered, exited, studied, felt. Theatre's strength is that its raw material is us, people. There's no leap into another medium – into paper or canvas or piano. Theatre deals with what we have to hand – our bodies and minds. This means that it can be excruciatingly bad – it's hard to gauge distance on the metaphorical weight of ourselves – but it also means that, at its best, theatre speaks totally to how we are and how we could be.

This human potential for theatre exists as much in its form as in the stories it tells. I think I agree that a revolutionary action placed in a reactionary form defeats any radical objective – and vice versa. Form is the deepest communicator. Form is the here and now. It is the pattern that integrates most keenly with our everyday life. It's the people you cast in your play, the colour of their skin, their gender, their bodies, their relationship to power. It's how language is used; how space is democratised; how uncertainty and ambivalence is accepted – or not; it's a reflection of an aesthetic sensibility that is continuously changing. I don't want stories about crisis as much as I want crisis refracted through form.

***Adler & Gibb* premiered at the Royal Court Theatre, London in June 2014**

The children swing their legs on the chairs. The student delivers the presentation. The older woman stands with the gun. The young couple arrives at the house. The house is returning to nature. A movie is being made. The truth is being plundered. But the house is still lived in and the spirit to resist is strong.

Janet Adler and Margaret Gibb were conceptual artists working in New York at the end of the last century. They were described by art critic Dave Hickey as the 'most ferociously uncompromising voice of their generation'. With Adler's death in 2004, however, the compromise began.

Adler & Gibb tells the story of a raid – on a house, a life, a reality and a legacy.

Louise *enters, transformed into Adler – clothes, wig, make-up.*

She is carrying a shovel in one hand.

A moment between 'Adler' and **Gibb**.

. . .

Louise *and* **Gibb** *turn in on each other.*

The performances are gradually becoming more dimensional.

Gibb Oh, darling. Were you just upstairs? Was it you, darling? Was that you clumping around? Is that where you were, all this time? All those years. Ten years, is it now? I thought you were dead. Why didn't you come down? Were you playing with me? What you got in your hand? You dig yourself out with that? Is that it? You clever girl! I was going to. I promise I was going to. Here, Boy. Come see who's back! Boy sat by you for weeks, he did. Look how old he's gotten. There's only us two left. Oh, honey. Honey. This place has gone bad. A man is bleeding here. When you went. Why didn't I come with you? Oh God, oh God. I'm sorry. Let's get out of this place. Let's start again. Take me back, will you? Take me with you? I've been missing you. You been missing me? Oh, God, honey, I'm not dressed right. I've let myself go. Don't look at me, don't. I'm a mess. A mess! I'm ashamed. You still love me, don't you? Look, Boy, look who's here!

The child has come on and now approaches **Louise**. *The child looks at* **Louise**. *The child looks at* **Gibb**.

Gibb What?

She reaches out to **Louise** *and then suddenly recoils. The child sits down.*

Gibb Wait.

Did I invite you?

Louise In high school I had your picture on my wall.

Gibb Well?

Louise I was obsessed with you.

Gibb Did I?

Louise You and Janet –

Gibb Let me see.

Louise – gave me such hope –

Gibb Racking my brain, here.

Louise – the way you lived.

Gibb I forget.

Louise I adored you.

Gibb It has slipped my mind.

Louise I have your tattoo.

She shows her forearm.

Gibb Are you listening?

Louise Look!

Gibb Mute, am I?

Louise I freaking studied you!

Gibb Did I send you an invitation?

Louise I dressed like you.

Gibb Did I request the pleasure of your company?

Louise I went to pieces when Janet died.

Gibb Did you RSVP?

Louise I can't believe I am standing here with you.

Gibb Did you even think?

Louise We thought you were dead!

Gibb Well?

Louise I was your biggest fan!

Gibb What happened to you?

Louise I want to give this back to you.

Gibb Well?

Louise My gift.

Gibb Gift?

Louise I've come to rescue you, Margaret.

Gibb Did I send out a distress signal? Did I? I forget. Did I send up a flare? Did I leave a trail of breadcrumbs? Did I international SOS save my soul? Remind me? Did I at any moment – to your recollection – present myself as in any way, any conceivable way, being in need of rescue? Is that your jacket?

Louise Yes.

Gibb Would you take that jacket off?

Louise There's nothing on the label. (*She calls.*) Sam.

Gibb Where did you find it?

Louise I'm not going to damage it. (*She calls.*) Sam.

Gibb It's not yours. It's not yours. Help. Stop thief. Rape. Rape.

What gift?

Louise Watch.

She adopts a slight Austrian accent – a perfect impersonation.

'It will all end with us. You and me. You know that too, don't you? We will be like climbing partners roped together. If one of us goes, then they will pull the other with them. Gladly down into the crevasse.'

Gibb Who told you that?

Louise It's in / a letter.

Gibb Was that a letter to you, was it? Was it?

Louise That / letter was –

Gibb Was that letter a public letter?

Louise You didn't go down the crevasse, / did you?

Gibb A letter for the / public domain?

Louise She fell on her own, / didn't she?

Gibb Written for a newspaper, / was it?

Louise You watched / her?

Gibb Posted outside the town hall? / Was it?

Louise You pushed / her down?

Gibb A parish notice, was it? / An editorial?

Louise Couldn't cope out here?

Gibb You'd like that, would you, your most private, pinkest, tenderest – small bird, small bird, small fragile – stolen from you, slammed down onto the slab, the block, poked at and paraded. Butchered by a puppet, a dummy, a cartoon rapist.

Louise Couldn't cope with her success? Eaten up with envy, was it? An act of violence? A miscalculation? A regrettable outburst? That's what they say.

Gibb They.

Louise Why are you still alive?

A child substitutes the shovel with another object. A plastic lobster, for example.

Gibb How old you meant to be?

Louise Who?

Gibb Dressed like this.

Louise When we first see her she's thirty-three.

Gibb You thirty-three?

Louise They age me. (*She calls.*) Sam.

Gibb Ha.

Louise The scene is when you first – When you first get together. '76. In the loft on West 10th. The neon sign outside the window. Janet wrote about it. There's a glimpse of her on film on that night. Before she gets you home. She's by the window in a gallery. One of the few films we've got of her in the early days, before she became who she was. She's talking to a man – Perryman, we think – God, you should know!

Gibb I don't remember.

Louise She's animated, angry even. It's a private view. Her hair up. Pencil behind the ear. It's when you meet. She looks like this. She takes you back to the apartment. And we see her on the film – and then she turns and walks towards the door. She turns and walks. See?

She walks.

This is the first time the fictional space is broken with a completed physical action.

Gibb What do you want me to say?

Louise It would be an honour, Margaret, if you would just – just watch and be open. We are having difficulties finding her. I have undertaken a lot of work. Invested a lot of time and energy. This is such a bonus to have you – we didn't think – It would mean a lot to me and to this film to – to have your / validation.

Gibb Okay. Oh, I get it now. I think you have made a profound mistake. Yes, a grave error, an error of judgement.

Louise Margaret.

Gibb No help here. No help for me. No help for you. No gift needed. Do not resuscitate. What is this? Some kind of joke? Some trick or treat? Dress up and scare me to death, is it? Break my heart, is it? This pastiche. This parody. This clown costume. This embarrassment. Have you not, despite your years, grown out of this? Where's your boyfriend?

Louise He's not my boyfriend.

Gibb Really? Bleeding his way around my house. Snaffling around like a hog. My private house. You cease this minute, you hear. You cease and desist.

Here, Boy.

She walks away. The child joins her.

Louise We're looking for the diaries.

Gibb *walks back.*

Gibb You have no / right.

Louise The notebooks, the journals she kept. She didn't burn them, right? She told Scott Berg she would be buried with them – with them and with other stuff. Is that right? Was that just words?

Gibb She spoke to no one.

Louise What's out there?

Gibb No one.

Louise Is there a shallow grave? More work? You want to tell us where that is? The more you tell us, the sooner we'll be gone. There are plenty of people who would give a lot to see those papers. To understand the last years of her life. Her death. To stop the rumours. Not least the rumours about you. You don't come across as very nice, Margaret, not in this film. Not here. Not in real life.

Gibb You don't know what happened.

Louise We still have time to change the script, to rewrite the ending.

Gibb Take your hands off me. Take your / hands off.

Louise Shut up. Shut up.

Gibb You're nothing like her.

A child executes a substitution – ending with the 'spade' as a pool noodle swim float, for example.

From this moment **Louise***'s accent is naturalised southern Californian with a hint of New Jersey.*

Louise In three weeks we start to make a motion picture, do you understand that? Now, that's a fact of life, you can't change that – the green light is on – that's happening whether you want it to or not. When that movie is released, whether you help us or not, I will become your lover. To all the world, I will *become* her. I won't only be the actress who played her, I will *be* her. Be her. The real Janet is a long time dead and buried in the yard now, that's distant history now. When they think of Janet Adler, they will think of me. Now we could go ahead without you. Or you could help me get it right. It's your call.

Gibb Who am I?

Louise What?

Gibb Who is me?

Louise In the film?

Gibb Do I even feature?

Louise Oh. She's beautiful.

Gibb I'm not beautiful.

Louise You're a perfect match. She would love to meet you. We can fly you over. As a consultant or advisor. Or you could be in it. A walk-on, a cameo. We'd put you up somewhere special. Get you out of this place. Clean it up. Straighten it up. How can you live in this chaos? This forest – this vegetation – is that a tree, is that a real tree? – how could you let this happen? This place could be quite a place. See, you're warming to the idea, hey, I can see it in your face. Or you could come now – we have an RV, a Winnebago. Whisk you away. The world would love to see you. God, you poor thing, stuck here, building this wall around you. See what happens when we take one brick away from that wall. See how good that feels? Margaret?

Gibb What if we don't want to be remembered.

Louise Everyone wants to be remembered.

Gibb Is that so?

Louise You made some of the most influential work of the late 20th century.

Gibb Not our intention.

Louise Then you should have thought about that when you were doing it.

Gibb How does it end?

Louise The movie?

Gibb What happens to me?

Louise We want to tell the truth.

Gibb (*to the dog*) Go to work.

The child/dog on stage 'attacks' **Louise**.

Louise *clubs the child/dog to 'death' with whatever she's holding in her hand – the swim float, for example. A savage and playful struggle. The child twitches and eventually lies still.*

Barber Shop Chronicles

Inua Ellams

Born in Nigeria, **Inua Ellams** is a poet, playwright and performer, graphic artist and designer. He is a Complete Works poet alumnus and facilitates workshops in creative writing where he explores reoccurring themes in his work – identity, displacement and destiny – in accessible, enjoyable ways for participants of all ages and backgrounds.

His awards include: Edinburgh Fringe First Award 2009, Liberty Human Rights Award, Live Canon International Poetry Prize, Kent and Sussex Poetry Competition, Magma Poetry Competition, Winchester Poetry Prize, Arts Council of England Award, Wellcome Trust Award, Black British Theatre Award and Hay Festival Medal for Poetry.

He has been commissioned by the Royal Shakespeare Company, National Theatre, Tate Modern, Louis Vuitton, Chris Ofili, and BBC Radio and Television. His poetry books include *Thirteen Fairy Negro Tales* and *Candy Coated Unicorn and Converse* (Flipped Eye) and *The Wire-Headed Heathen* (Akashic Books). His plays include *Black T-shirt Collection*, *The 14th Tale*, *Barber Shop Chronicles* and *Three Sisters* (Oberon). He founded The Midnight Run (an arts-filled, night-time, urban walking experience), The Rhythm and Poetry Party (The R.A.P Party) which celebrates poetry and hip hop, and Poetry + Film / Hack (P+F/H) which celebrates poetry and film.

What does the word 'crisis' mean to you in a theatrical sense?

In a theatrical sense, crisis means intense conflict; the point in a story when the protagonist's deepest self, or deepest sense of self, faces its gravest forces or forces that seem unsurmountable.

How do you feel theatre has the ability to represent/respond to global crises?

In various ways . . . by offering escapism, by showing parallels to the crises, by metaphorically playing out aspects of the crises, or by directly mirroring the crises . . . all of which helps us think or meditate on what we are going through and how to respond to it.

Why did you pick this specific scene? What is this scene doing at this point of the play?

I chose this scene because it is one of the most self-contained to be found in *Barber Shop Chronicles*. This scene follows the first real conversation about political fatherhood in London, England. There, an older barber mounts a passionate defence of the divisive figure of former president of Zimbabwe Robert Mugabe to his younger client. In this scene set in Zimbabwe, that defence is ripped apart and the intergenerational codes of conduct that are often adhered to in heated African arguments and ignored. The overall crisis in patrilineal relationships mounts.

How does this scene speak beyond the wider context of the play?

Beyond the play, the scene is emblematic of the cross-generational and global criticisms of the responses to the pandemic. Within the pandemic, there are socio-economic forces at play, there is distrust of those in power, of those who returned to their home countries, of racial elements in how indigenous remedial breakthroughs are reported by foreign press. In the scene, the crises is ultimately unresolved, and all epidemiological studies suggest this will be so for the pandemic.

As a writer, do you feel a point of crisis is always necessary in a play to create/maintain/sustain drama?

No, I do not. I think tension is, but there are others ways to create tension.

Does theatre as a form allow for a more effective exploration of crisis in terms of what can be explored, presented and communicated to an audience, in relation to other creative forms?

I don't think so. I work in many other creative forms and explore crisis in many other ways. I find poetry to allow the greatest space for experimenting with crisis, and representing crisis. Often there is conflict between subject matter and form, between lines and space, between line breaks and syntax that create really thrilling uses of language all of which heightens suspense and crisis.

When constructing a play how do you effectively boil down larger global themes that could otherwise be overwhelming for characters within 'their world' so that they can find room to resonate?

I try to think of the most unlikely characters to be affected by a subject matter or the theme of a play, and then I try to see the world through their eyes. Thinking this way gives space for the character to come naturally to a larger global theme, and the way it affects them will be specific and deeply personal.

What do you feel is the biggest threat to the creation of new drama and plays given the current global crisis? Do we need theatre now more than ever?

The biggest threat is the notion that we have to create plays that tackle the global crisis head on. That will only produce terrible plays. Great art comes from mediation and distance, and we need both to know how to write about what we are going through. We are still in the eye of the storm, we do not know the size of the storm, how long it will last for, what damage it has caused and what will be its legacy. We barely understood where we were, and we do not know where we are going yet. The togetherness of experiencing storytelling in theatres is what makes theatre special and we cannot do that. I think we need art more than ever, but not theatre in the traditional sense. The world must settle first, and theatre must evolve to exist in that world.

***Barber Shop Chronicles* premiered at the National Theatre, London in June 2017**

Barber Shop Chronicles is a generously funny, heart-warming and insightful new play set in five African cities, Johannesburg, Harare, Kampala, Lagos, Accra, and in London.

Inspired in part by the story of a Leeds barber, the play invites the audience into a unique environment where the banter may be barbed, but the truth always telling. The barbers of these tales are sages, role models and father figures who keep the men together and the stories alive.

Scene Nine

Characters

Tinashe, *Zimbabwean. Early twenties.*
Dwain, *Zimbabwean. Mid thirties.*

// 15:00. A ceiling fan swirls above. Bob Marley & the Wailers' 'One Love' plays. **Tinashe** *pours cream from a giant tub into smaller bottles. He doesn't have enough space on the tables; we laugh as he creates a mess of things.* **Dwain** *enters.*

Dwain Did you watch the match? We destroyed Barcelona!

Tinashe Ah! Dwain! Just the man I'm looking for.

Dwain Oooh, what's all this?

Tinashe New delivery straight from Kampala! Anti-balding cream made with local Ugandan herbs. Ancient formula.

Dwain Are you trying to sell me one?

Tinashe Huh?

Dwain Am I balding? Why am I the man you're looking for?

Tinashe (*laughs*) No. My cousin Tanaka is moving back from London on Wednesday. I'm trying to prepare him for the change, and you just moved back too.

Dwain Does he have a British passport? What's his job?

Tinashe Ya British passport. He writes about politics a bit.

Dwain Yo! vaMugabe doesn't like people from the West.

They always lying about him. If he says he is a writer, he won't get past the border.

Tinashe (*laughs*) That's exactly the kinda stuff I need!

Dwain Okay. But haircut? On the house?

Tinashe Yeah.

Dwain So listen, I wanted to talk about your party anyway.

// **Dwain** *sits by the radio and tunes into Chimurenga music.*

Tinashe I bet you don't have parties in Joburg . . . is that why you left and came back to Harare?

Dwain (*laughs*) I came back because our music industry has grown. I wanted to do hip-hop when I was twenty-one but there were no spaces, so I left. Now, things have changed. More cash, more venues, and now we play local music! I play the same gigs here that I did in Joburg. Here, I make more. Don't know how long it's gonna last, but for now . . .

Tinashe It's good?

Dwain Ya! So much music! But the world doesn't know.

Tinashe Why?

Dwain Because Zimbabwe is bashed by media outside, because vaMugabe took land from white people.

Tinashe To a returnee, how d'you explain what happened?

Dwain We took back our land.

Beat.

Tinashe That's it?

Dwain (*laughs*) Plain and simple.

Tinashe People were killed.

Dwain Yah.

Tinashe White people.

Dwain So?

Beat.

Tinashe Tanaka has white friends. They believe / that

Dwain White *and* black people died. Both. We wanted our land back and got it! See, we are natural farmers. Before, most of us owned land and our food came from that land.

This is our culture, like Kenyans are cattle herders, that's their culture. And yes, you know, our crops failed; but after generations without our land there were bound to be teething problems, you know, yet they were ridiculing us and vaMugabe.

Tinashe My mother told me.

Dwain VaMugabe has eight degrees and they think he is stupid. He is struggling on the global stage, that's why I'm making Chimurenga music. Chimurenga means struggle / and I want

Tinashe (*sigh*) I know Dwain. You tell everyone.

Dwain At your party, you weren't playing Chimurenga.

Tinashe It wasn't the right vibe.

Dwain If you played it, it would have become the vibe. We have to support each other. You really disappointed me, your party was shit! Young people should play our own music. My songs are all about / our attempts

Tinashe We can play what we want!

Dwain We should play who we are.

// **Tinashe** *turns off the radio.*

Tinashe At the party, people were asking *who's the old guy hassling DJs, telling them what to play.* If you don't like the music, go!

// **Dwain** *pulls away sharply.*

Dwain I'm trying to restore national identity / to our

Tinashe By what?! By plying us with your shit songs?

Pretending to care? You left, Dwain! You left! When things got tough, you left. Things are better, you've come back, acting like you care, wanna tell us who we are? We don't want your dictatorship, Mugabe is enough!

Dwain Before I left young people would never talk to elders like this.

Tinashe The older a man get, the faster he could run as a boy.

// **Dwain** *stands up.*

Dwain I don't have to listen to this. There're other barbers / who won't insult

Tinashe Go! It's just three o'clock! More clients will come!

Don't need your money!

// **Dwain** *storms off.*

Tinashe It was a free haircut anyway!

A History of Falling Things

James Graham

James Graham is a multi-award-winning playwright and screenwriter.

His play *This House* gained critical acclaim, enjoyed a sell-out run at the National Theatre's Olivier in 2013 and its 2017 West End revival was Olivier-nominated. It was chosen by popular vote as the best play of the 2010s by Methuen Drama.

James created theatre history when his two plays *Ink*, about the early days of Rupert Murdoch, and *Labour of Love*, a romantic political comedy, played in theatres next to each other in the West End in 2017. James won an Olivier Award in 2018 for *Labour of Love* and *Ink* transferred to Broadway in 2019, receiving six Tony Award nominations.

James's play *Quiz* (Chichester Minerva Theatre/West End) became an Easter ITV drama in 2020. Prior to that his television film *Brexit: An Uncivil War* (Channel 4/HBO) was nominated for a 2019 Emmy Award.

James's play *The Vote* (Donmar Warehouse) aired in real time on TV in the final ninety minutes of the 2015 polling day and was BAFTA-nominated.

What does the word 'crisis' mean to you in a theatrical sense?

For me I think ultimately it's the arrival at a moment in a play where a decision has to be made, either for a character or – in the case of a lot of what I like to write about – for the institution or system you're representing. You're building a character with wants and needs facing obstacles and dilemmas and you've dragged them kicking and screaming towards a crossroads where they face a specific difficulty, ideally both externally and internally, and they must now decide whether to overcome it or succumb to it.

How do you feel theatre has the ability to represent/respond to global crises?

It's live for one thing, so unlike multimillion dollar films or heavily produced television it should be able to respond to events that occurred that day later on that night. Although, I'd argue, just because theatre can be that responsive, doesn't mean it always *should*. Because theatre's language isn't as bound up in the hard naturalism of screen drama or the literal truth of journalism, it can probe the crisis in a more artful and inventive, and also a more humane and empathetic way. Quiz was, I hope, a fairly playful and mischievous television drama the stage-play version was a much more expressionist, interactive, creative, un-naturalistic response to the same themes, the themes of truth and justice and perception and manipulation. It required what theatre should always require to work – an audience present, live, engaging with it collectively as a physical community

Why did you pick this specific scene? What is this scene doing at this point of the play?

It's three little scene-lets. Where Jacqui and Robin have decided to have an online date and it results in them deciding to meet each other in the real world and face their fears. I think that is the real moment of crisis in this play, for those two characters they have arrived at a point where they can't continue in the direction that they are going which is actually directionless. They're in a purgatory of their own making; they're too frightened to change anything. I think like most great crises, either personal or institutional, you arrive at a moment when their previous existence has become unsustainable and they have to decide to go left or right, up or down, this or that, and so they face their fears of going outside and something falling from the sky. Which of course as an audience we suspect is more than a fear of something falling on their heads – it's a fear of intimacy and of being brave and being hurt as they decide they're going to go for it.

How does this scene speak beyond the wider context of the play?

The political world that this play was born out of, regardless of the desire to write a very odd bizarre sort of romantic comedy, was the world of terror and coming out of the 2007 bomb attacks in London and the fear that placed on people. It was to use fear as the impediment to two people getting together rather than what might be the traditional star-crossed lovers impediment which might be to do with class or status or warring families or geographical divide. The impediment here is how the fear of something – a terror attack, something falling from the sky, or being emotional vulnerable with another person – can inhibit you. That was the mood in the air at the time of writing the play.

As a writer, do you feel a point of crisis is always necessary in a play to create/maintain/sustain drama?

I do because I am a narrative writer. I really love story and I really love building towards a moment where you test your characters to the extremes, or you show the worlds that you are representing on stage at a crossroads where they start to shake under the pressure of that, whether that's the Houses of Parliament in *This House* where you put it under the most extreme pressures and often it will either improve or it will collapse. That's the same with characters and people. I think narratively an audience really wants you to put your characters through the ringer. With *Ink*, Larry Lamb the editor of *The Sun*, the decision he had to make whether or not to print a story is a moment of crisis in that play. In that moment you're trying to represent both the general dilemma of the news industry in one man's personal moment of crisis.

When constructing a play how do you effectively boil down larger global themes that could otherwise be overwhelming for characters within 'their world' so that they can find room to resonate?

I don't like thinking in terms of 'theme' which sounds very worthy and grand; for me I think in terms of anxieties. *A History of Falling Things* on a personal level is about my anxieties around intimacy in relationships both for me as individual – the writer – but also on a societal level, a society that has become more atomised and less together. In something like *Quiz* the anxiety was about truth and how vulnerable and fragile mutually accepted facts are to manipulation and the distortion of reality particularly today and particularly now. I don't necessarily have the answers or a point of view always but I enjoy trying to interrogate contemporary anxieties and represent those through narrative and a character's journey. The greatest characters on stage often exist on the level of metaphor; they represent metaphorically the dilemma that you're trying to represent. One of my favourite examples will always be John Proctor in *The Crucible*. He represents on a beautifully metaphorical plane all the contradictions and problems and challenges and opportunities of the birthing of America in one tortured man.

What do you feel is the biggest threat to the creation of new drama and plays given the current global crisis?

The biggest impediment is exactly what makes theatre so brilliant and beautiful and special and that's what a virus prevents the most – being together in a collective community that we're all deeply missing in a pandemic but also deeply weary and fearful of. That is theatre's USP – that's why watching a *Star Wars* movie on your phone can never replicate watching something live in real time, breathing the same oxygen as the people who are making the story – that's the reason it has survived for 2000 years and the reason why I think it will survive another 2000 years, but it's getting people back into the habit of being willing to do that and to experience something in that way.

***A History of Falling Things* premiered at Clwyd Theatr Cymru, Wales in April 2009**

Prisoners of their fear of falling things – keraunothetophobiacs – Jacqui and Robin are restricted to living indoors. When they meet online a relationship begins which forces them to confront their fear and discover what's real in their lives and what really matters.

In the centre space. A firework goes off. And then another. And then more.

Jacqui *leans in, watching from her room.* **Robin** *from his.*

Robin Can you see them?

Jacqui Yes! YES! They're beautiful! How did you . . .?

Robin They're, um, from a box, you just, you just, light and run. Huh.

Jacqui So you went outside? Into your garden?

Robin I. Well. I. Yeah. I. Ran outside. And then, huh, and then ran back in.

Jacqui Robin, that's . . . that's amazing. Well done.

Robin Well. It's your birthday in, (*Checks his watch.*) ooh, eleven minutes. So.

Jacqui Thank you. (*Watches.*) So that's where you live. Over there.

Robin Yeah. Yeah, this is where I live. So. What do you think? Give it a go?

Jacqui (*pause*) I've been doing. So well, Robin –

Robin Just to see. Just so I can show you. How it could work.

Pause.

Jacqui (*smiles*) OK.

Blackout on the rooms. The fireworks continue for a while, before fizzling out . . .

Jacqui *in her room, glammed up in a dress.* **Robin** *in his house, wearing a suit. Each has half a dining table in their rooms that are split at the cut-off point – two parts of the same whole. Candles are lit.*

Robin *already has a plate of food at his table.*

Jacqui (*twirling*) Well?

Robin You look amazing.

Knock at her bedroom. **Jimmy** *stands holding a thermos bag and a bottle of wine.*

Jacqui And who could this be? (*Answering.*) Well, hello, sir.

Jimmy Good evening, madam. I will be your waiter for this evening. May I present to you your meal?

Jacqui Why, thank you. (*Smelling.*) Hmm, lovely.

Jimmy And. (*Sprays her wrist with aftershave.*) Your date wishes you to know how he smells this evening.

Jacqui (*sniffing her wrist*) Hmm, gorgeous. Wow. Very nice.

Jimmy The gentleman also requested that I deliver this. (*Kisses her on the cheek.*) With his best wishes.

If you need anything just call and I'm only thirty to forty minutes away.

Jacqui Thanks, Jimmy.

Jimmy You look stunning.

He leaves. **Jacqui** *goes to the table, removing a plate from the heat-sealed bag, removing the cling film and sitting at the table with the wine.* **Robin** *also sits.*

Robin Shall we?

Jacqui I can't believe you cooked this, looks amazing.

Robin Is it still warm?

Jacqui I'm sure it's fine.

Robin Wine?

Jacqui Thank you. Shall I pour myself?

Robin Uh, if you wouldn't mind.

Jacqui There. (*Tasting the food.*) Mm. *Mm*. Wow. Well done you.

Robin 'S all right.

Jacqui It's better than all right, stop putting yourself down.

Robin It's nice not to just cook for one. For once. Happy birthday.

Jacqui So. How was your day at work today, darling, all right?

Robin Oh, fine. Fine. Got the first draft of my next book to the agent, you know. You?

Jacqui Oh, I decided to work from home today.

Robin Really?

Jacqui Hmm. So. When are you going to tell me about your new book?

Robin Ugh. Nah. I'll only make it sound rubbish.

Jacqui No, you won't. Come on.

Robin Really. Honestly. No. I, I don't like . . . before it's done, I –

Jacqui False modesty. What's it called?

Robin (*sighs*) It, it's called . . . no. OK. It's called . . . (*Pause. Sighs.*) *Poor Poor Pluto.* And. It's about . . . well, it's, the characters are. Um. Are the planets. In the solar system. And, (see I'm making it sound) . . . and, uh, Pluto. Is the main character.

And all it is, is he gets told, by the others, that he isn't a proper planet any more.

Jacqui Awh.

Robin Exactly. So. And he's always been kind of skirting around on the peripheries of the, of the proverbial playground as it were anyway, but *now* . . . Well, officially he, it was downgraded to, erm . . . Well, and don't read too much into this, but now I've said that, of course you're going . . . uh, to a satellite. Huh. Coinc– oddly enough. Like the moon of something else. So condemned into a supporting role. Doing what satellites do. Orbiting around the main body. Watching. But never . . . getting involved. Just watching.

Jacqui Huh. Where *do* you get your ideas from? (*Smiles.*) I hope it's a success for you.

Robin Y-we-ye-well . . . (Shh.) Thank you.

Music pumps out. **Robin** *and* **Jacqui** *spin away their chairs, brush themselves down, face each other and count themselves in. They begin a jive – despite the distance between them, they could almost be dancing together. They laugh and giggle but continue, mock-seriously. Finishing with a flourish.*

Late night. **Jacqui** *is sprawled on the bed.* **Robin** *in his room.*

Jacqui You know, if the writing thing doesn't work out, which I'm sure it will, but if it doesn't, I reckon as a chef you'd do bloody well. Or even a professional dancer.

Robin Well, I'll need a partner.

Jacqui You went to a lot of trouble.

Robin Not really.

Jacqui No you did. (*Beat. As mock-American girl.*) 'This was my bestest birthday ever!'

Robin Hmm.

Jacqui *smells her wrist. Smiles. Smells it again.*

Jacqui Well, I'd invite you in for coffee, but . . .

Robin *gasps playfully.*

Jacqui But I'm not that kind of girl.

Robin And I'm not that kind of boy.

Jacqui Good. So. (*Standing.*) I guess . . . (*Wobbling on her feet.*) Whoop.

Robin You all right?

Jacqui Yep. Yep. These heels. It's been a while.

Robin Oh, it's the heels.

Jacqui Yes. It is. So. (*Sighs.*) So. I guess this is where we leave it.

Robin *smiles weakly, and nods. Long, heavy pause.*

Jacqui Thank you, Robin, for a . . . for a really nice birthday.

Robin Hmm . . . It isn't enough, is it?

Pause.

Jacqui It's been a lovely / evening.

Robin It isn't enough. Where from here, what next? Tomorrow? It isn't enough. (*Pause.*) I . . . I don't want to lose this.

Jacqui We don't have to lose this. I just don't think it can . . . I don't think it can be anything *more* than this. If it *is* this. Do you see? I'm sorry.

Robin Then . . . then . . . then let's . . . let's do it.

Jacqui Do what?

Robin Let, let's, let's . . . let, let's, let's meet. I'll, I'll . . . I'll meet you.

Jacqui What do you mean?

Robin Let's do this. Let, let's meet. I'll, I can, I'll l-l-leave. I'll come to you. And you to me. And, and we'll, we'll. Meet.

Pause.

Jacqui You'll . . .?

Robin Let's meet. Let's just do it. Let's just try, I'm . . . I'm willing to . . . (shit!) I'll try. Now. Soon, now.

Beat.

Jacqui (*beat; laughs*) Seriously? What? No. Seriously?

Robin Yes?

Jacqui All right, then. (*Beat; laughs.*) Oh my God!

Robin (*laughs; cries a bit; laughs*) Shit.

Jacqui How? When? Oh my God, no. Really? No!

Robin Let's – we need – let's . . . I don't know, find somewhere. Halfway between. But it, it has to be soon, otherwise, I'll . . . shit. Jesus! Has to be soon. Has to be –

Jacqui Tomorrow?

Robin OK.

Pause. **Jacqui** *squeals, excited and terrified.*

Robin (*laughs, drops to his knees, stands again*) Oh God, oh God, oh shit, uh –

Jacqui But, but *you*, you haven't been out in –

Robin Well, I, I, I, I . . . I could, I could do with the, the, huh, the fresh air. Uh . . .

Jacqui No. No, we're going to wake up tomorrow and not do it. I know it.

Robin No.

Jacqui It's because we've been drinking.

Robin No, no. I will. I want to. I can. I will. We just need to plan it.

Robin (*speaking out, getting changed as he does*) I don't believe a word I'm saying. Just so you know. I'm just a bystander, watching the words come out my mouth, and thinking, 'Christ, you're on your own there, mate. Enjoy.' And I'm just humouring him. But things get away from you, and once you're in the thing, the carriage, and the bar comes down over your lap and you're setting off up the roller coaster there isn't much you can do, is there? Except scream your tits off, of course.

Jacqui *in her room, changed to go out.* **Robin** *the same in his. He taps on his computer. On the screen at the back, a street map of the local area.*

Jacqui You OK?

Robin No. You?

Jacqui No, not even a little bit.

Robin Good. At least we're on the same page. Huh.

Jacqui Oh my God . . .

Robin I've got your mobile number, if there's a problem, I'll find, find a phone box. Do they still exist? Round here? Phone boxes?

Jacqui Uh, yeah, s'pose. Shit.

Robin So. One o'clock. Under the bridge. (*Pointing at the map.*) By the side of the park.

Jacqui One o'clock. Under the bridge. One o'clock. That's half an hour. That's fine. Ha. Under the bridge. Strong, sturdy bridge.

Smiles nervously. Stops. Deep breath.

I w-wish you had a, a mobile.

Robin Nev– never needed one. (*Attempting a jokey tone, but failing.*) Plus they, they attract satellites, so . . .

Pause.

Jacqui How do I look?

Robin Fine. Is it warm outside? This too much?

Jacqui Dunno. You got everything?

Robin I don't . . . know what I need. Oh God.

Goes to be sick. Gags a bit. Gathers himself.

I'm. Sorry, if . . . if I don't make it –

Jacqui Don't. You will. Don't say that. It's just this first part that's the worst. Once we're out. Once we're . . . maybe we should have done taxis.

Robin No! No, we – if we did that, then what? Get the taxis to take us back to one of ours and then what? Get them to wait, and take one of us back, and then . . . no, if we're doing it, then . . . then we're bloody –

Jacqui No, you're right. (You're right.) Huh. Just think in, in about five minutes' time we'll be as close to each other as we are to home.

Robin Yeah. Yeah. A bit like what the Russian army used to do.

Jacqui Is it?

Robin Yeah.

Jacqui Oh. That's good then.

Robin Whenever they were invaded, from the west, they, they, the Russians, they'd retreat back. Back and back into their own country, sort of scorching the land as they, they went, so the enemy couldn't get any food or shelter. And eventually they'd been lured so far in, the enemy were just too far from home to go back, but going forward there was just more, uh, more barren land, and so they were just kinda stuck.

Jacqui Oh. What happened, then?

Robin Well. They all, they all died. So.

Jacqui Oh. OK. 'S a good story.

Robin Thank you.

Jacqui My answer machine! Need to record a message, for the first time in . . . (*Presses button on answer machine. It beeps.*) Uh, hello, you've reached Jacqui's phone. Um . . . ha-hard as it may be to believe, I'm actually out. So. So leave a message. Or call my mobile, erm. If, if you don't have my mobile number then, uh . . . well, then, there's a reason for that, thanks, bye. (*Presses the button.*) So-o-o . . .

Robin So. (*Sighs heavily.*) I do, I really do, erm . . . I really do think that, that I . . . Jacqui, I really do believe that in the past months I've started to fa– that I am in, in . . . or I least could be one day, in, in lo–

Jacqui Wait. Wait. Save it. For face to face.

Robin Face to face. (*Nods.*) Huh. Face to face. Just the thought of being able to . . . to touch you. Not, no, not in, in that –

Robin I didn't mean –

Robin I mean . . . just . . . for you to just be real. For you to just be real.

Jacqui I'm going to turn you off now.

Robin No, wait, don't, why?!

Jacqui I don't want you to see me leave.

Robin What, no, I need to see you go otherwise –

Jacqui I need to . . . (*Sighs.*) 'put' something else on, but I don't want you to see it –

Robin Don't be silly, I –

Jacqui Fine! Just . . .

She retrieves a London Beefeater's hat and puts it on.

Jacqui But don't ask me why, it just makes me feel better. Protected. Better.

Robin I wish I had something. Oh.

He grabs an umbrella and shows her. They smile.

(*Deep breath.*) So.

Jacqui So. You could write about this one day. Our own little adventure story.

Jacqui One to tell you all. When we get back.

Robin Yeah. If it ends well.

Jacqui Course it will end well. How would it end?

Robin I dunno. How will it end?

Jacqui With a, a happy ending. I hope. In colour.

Robin Yeah. Course. Happy ending would be good.

Jacqui Under the bridge, one o'clock.

Robin Under the bridge. One o'clock. (*Deep breath.*) Later, skater.

Jacqui (*smiles*) In a bit, shit.

Robin *goes to his door.* **Jacqui** *to hers. They open them.* **Jacqui** *rests her head against the frame.* **Robin** *weakens and drops to his knees, but quickly struggles back up. Beat. They both bolt out, screaming,* **Robin** *opening the umbrella as he goes . . .*

Dim lights up on **Jacqui***'s room. The phone rings. After a few seconds it goes to voicemail, and we hear the first moments of her recorded message.*

Lights down.

Dim lights up on **Jacqui***'s room as she enters. She turns the light on.*

She stands motionless for a while. She takes her shoes off. Tosses them down.

She looks over at **Robin***'s room, in semi-darkness still . . .*

She notices the red light flashing on her machine. She presses play. It beeps.

Answering machine You have . . . one . . . message.

Lights down.

Robin*'s house.* **Robin** *is sitting on the floor.* **Lesley** *sits nearby. Silence.*

Lesley Did you have that casserole in the end? All right, was it?

Pause. **Robin** *nods.*

Lesley So you tried the path thing, then, did you? That's what this is about?

Well, that's wonderful, that is. Well done, love. How far did you get?

Robin End of the path.

Lesley Right to the end?

Robin And a bit further.

Lesley And a bit further?! To where?

Robin Past the tree.

Lesley Past the *tree*?! Well that's wonderful, that is. Well done.

Robin It wasn't wonderful.

Lesley Now don't you put yourself down, Robin, don't you put yourself down, that's marvellous, that's more than marvellous, that's flippin' miraculous, that, well done.

Robin I was meant to go further.

Lesley What happened?

Robin I was meant to go all the way to her.

Under the bridge.

Screaming, off. Getting closer.

Jacqui *arrives at speed, wearing her Beefeater hat. She hits the floor. She stands, still screaming, but now happy, giddy, jumping up and down, clapping and squealing.*

Jacqui Argh – I – did – it, I bloody did it! I . . . I . . . argh!

She slowly gathers herself, and looks around for any sign of **Robin**. *The distant sound of a phone ringing. The opening of* **Jacqui***'s voicemail . . . as lights rise nearby on:*

A phone box. **Robin** *leaning against the side, catching his breath. Phone to his ear.*

Even though he is clearly far apart from **Jacqui**, *here they appear quite close.* **Robin** *is watching her. The message on* **Jacqui***'s answer machine ends, followed by the beep.*

Robin (*speaking into the phone*) Jacqui. (Jacqui.)

He leans out with the receiver, watching her. He rests his head against the side.

(*Sighs.*) I'm, erm . . . I'm in a phone box. And I can see you. You're waiting for me.

I'm, um . . . uh . . . I'm, I'm so sorry. (*Sighs. Groans.*) I'm so sorry.

Uh, you see. What's happened is. (What's happened is.)

The line beeps. He inserts coins.

Erm. Ha. I got here! I got here, isn't that – I didn't think I would and I nearly didn't but I did and it was hell, it was hell on earth, but I did, and I just kept running and I got here and . . . and I was afraid. I was really – but I . . . for as long as I can remember, I've been afraid. Uh, which isn't good. Huh. Erm. It isn't good to be, to be this afraid. Of things. I don't think. But, but being brave, as I understand it, being brave . . . it, it doesn't mean not being afraid, it means doing it, doing it in spite of being . . . I'm rambling, now, the point is. Jacqui.

Huh.

The point. Is.

That I've been so focused on, on . . . on things falling from the sky and, and beating that . . . (*Pause.*) I'm sorry. What am I saying? I'm saying. That there's something more frightening now than, than falling satellites.

The line beeps. He inserts coins.

It's been such a long time. Since anyone. Um. Cared about me, uh, in that way. If, if ever. And I, uh . . . I suppose I'm a little bit concerned about that now. Actually. Huh. That 'responsibility'. Um. Of, of being . . . Worth it. And seeing you here. Standing only, only yards away. Well. You're real. And.

Erm. And I'm not sure I can handle that. I'm a, a . . . huh . . . I'm a bystander, Jacqui. It, that's all I know. (That's all I know.)

He leans his head against the side. Hits his head against the side. Comes back up.

You. Wouldn't, uh . . . you wouldn't like me. In real life. Very much, I'm . . . I'm not one of those kinds of people that people really like. And I don't want to, to, lose . . . the thing we had. But, you know like all good things . . . well, you know, what, what goes up. Ey? (What goes up.)

He makes to replace the receiver, but stops, looking at **Jacqui** *again.*

Robin You, you really do look . . . really very good, though. You know. In the face.

So good I, I can hardly breathe, actually.

The line beeps. He makes to replace the receiver, but has a quick beat.

Oh and, uh, I love you.

He replaces the receiver. He watches **Jacqui***. He looks up at the sky, and exits at speed.* **Jacqui** *stands waiting under the arch. The lights fade out on her. Blackout.*

Lions and Tigers

Tanika Gupta

Over the past twenty-five years, **Tanika Gupta** has written over twenty-five stage plays that have been produced in major theatres across the UK and has written extensively for BBC Radio drama. Some of her theatre credits include: *A Doll's House* (Lyric Hammersmith); *Red Dust Road* – adaptation of Jackie Kay's memoir (NT Scotland); *Bones* (Central School for Speech and Drama); *Hobson's Choice* (Manchester Royal Exchange); *Lions and Tigers* (Sam Wanamaker Playhouse – winner of the James Tait Black Prize for Drama 2018); *A Short History of Tractors in Ukrainian* (Hull Truck Theatre); *A Midsummer Night's Dream* (Globe Theatre – dramaturg); *Anita and Me* (Birmingham Rep); *Love N Stuff* (Theatre Royal Stratford East); *The Empress* (Royal Shakespeare Company); *Wah! Wah! Girls* – A British Bollywood Musical (Sadler's Wells); *Mindwalking* (Bandbazi Theatre); *Great Expectations* (Watford Palace Theatre/English Touring Theatre); *Meet the Mukherjees* (Bolton Octagon Theatre); *White Boy* (National Youth Theatre/Soho Theatre); *Sugar Mummies* (Royal Court Theatre); *Gladiator Games* (Sheffield Crucible Theatre); *Hobson's Choice* (Young Vic); *Fragile Land* (Hampstead Theatre); *Inside Out* (Clean Break); *Sanctuary*, *The Good Woman of Setzuan* and *The Waiting Room* (National Theatre); *Skeleton* (Soho Theatre); and *A River Sutra* (Indoza).

Some of her television credits include: *Doctors*, *London Bridge*, *All About Me*, *EastEnders*, *Grange Hill*, *The Bill*, *Flight*, *Banglatown Banquet*, *Our Lives as Animals*, *The Fiancée* and *Bideshi*. Some of her radio credits include: *Trumpet*, *A Passage to India*, *Death of a Matriarch*, *The Home and the World*, *Emma*, *Writing the Century*, *Bindi Business*, *Song of the Road*, *The God of Small Things*, *Baby Farming* and *A Doll's House*.

In 2008 Tanika was awarded an MBE for Services to Drama and in 2016 was made a Fellow of the Royal Society of Literature. She has an honorary doctorate in the Arts from Chichester University and is an Honorary Fellow at Rose Bruford College and Central School of Speech and Drama. She won the James Tait Black Award in 2018 for her play *Lions and Tigers*.

What does the word `crisis' mean to you in a theatrical sense?

It is always very difficult for a playwright to say how we write, and what it is that we think of. However, I think for me crisis is very important because it elevates proceedings above the mundane. Characters need to be recognisable and rooted but we would not be interested in them unless something significant happens to them: unless they face conflict there will be no truly dramatic action. It is when characters face a crisis that they reveal themselves; it is when the story takes a twist that the drama unfolds. So the crisis in a play should always be personal – but it must also be political . . . it should have a larger resonance. I remember the late Stephen Jeffreys, a wonderful playwright and teacher, once told me that if you're going to write a play for the stage you have to say something about the state of the world we're living in. There's no point writing a play that's just about a relationship with nothing else around it, unless that relationship is set in a context and unless there is crisis. Drama comes to life through crisis.

Why did you pick this specific scene? What is this scene doing at this point of the play?

I would say that out of all of my `babies' *Lions and Tigers* is my favourite play. It's a terrible thing to say, isn't it? This scene in particular is the crisis point of the play where Dinesh Gupta, the Indian freedom fighter, comes right up face to face with the nasty side of the British Raj in the form of Tegart, who was the chief of police in Calcutta and was well known for using torture. Earlier on in the play we've seen a scene where Tegart has taught his men how to torture Indian `terrorists', so the stakes are already very high coming into this scene: at every moment you know that he could use any one of a number of torture techniques. There isn't actually much physical torture in the scene but this is a scene of sustained verbal combat between Dinesh and Tegart that is both intimately personal and deeply political: a young freedom fighter, Dinesh, making the case for nationalism and self-determination against a brutal Irish jailor who defends British colonial rule. Tegart attacks Dinesh on various fronts, one moment using racial stereotyping to tell him he is a weak Bengali man who should stick to poetry, the next moment humiliating him as a pathetic virgin, and then exploiting his emotions by telling Dinesh that his father has lost his job and his whole family will suffer. Perhaps most brutal is the way Tegart describes in vivid detail what it is like to be hanged in a physical sense. That is sustained mental torture which of course prefigures the end of the play when Dinesh is hanged. But throughout the scene

Dinesh remains strong and actually succeeds in getting inside Tegart's head, unnerving and destabilising him. Despite being in prison and apparently helpless, Dinesh wins the encounter. The key to the shifting dynamics of the scene are that these two central characters have different, contradictory wants and world-views.

How does this scene speak beyond the wider context of the play?

Dinesh Gupta was my grandfather's younger brother and I have heard family stories about him throughout my life, but it was when I read the two-volume handwritten journal that my grandfather wrote that I really understood the significance of his extraordinary short life. My grandfather interviewed everyone who knew Dinesh and collected the ninety-two letters that Dinesh had written from prison. It is a story I tried to write for the National Theatre over twenty years ago but I only really succeeded when revisiting it for the Globe, placing this personal story inside the wider political history of the time. In 1930 there was a huge conflict between Gandhi's non-violent civil disobedience movement and the Bengali leader Subhas Chandra Bose (Netaji) who supported armed struggle against British rule. Dinesh was a follower of Netaji. Laying out this conflict on a stage in the heart of London, looking across the river to St Paul's Cathedral, I kept thinking, 'My great-uncle would be quite pleased with this . . .' In this scene it is the British of course who resort to violence and the freedom fighter who wins the day with words. At a time when there is growing awareness of the importance of decolonising British education – to better reflect and analyse the crimes committed during the British Empire – this scene and this story become ever more important.

As a writer, do you feel a point of crisis is always necessary in a play to create/maintain/sustain drama?

I'm always thinking, 'How can I make this scene more dramatic?' In fact, in my teaching of undergraduates and masters students I'm constantly saying to people not only do your scenes have to be active and engaging but there has to be conflict. This can be done by putting your characters in extreme circumstances, tearing off their scabs so that you can see something fundamental about them. Crisis moments create turning points, unsettling moments of self-recognition or revelation. Without conflict or crisis most plays would be a bit boring.

Does theatre as a form allow for a more effective exploration of crisis in terms of what can be explored, presented and communicated to an audience, in relation to other creative forms?

I think all art forms represent crisis in some way but what makes theatre so special for me is that it's live action, you're watching it with a live audience. The actors can see the reaction of the audience during a moment of crisis and feed off it. And every night it will be different – not completely different – but small changes in the tone, rhythm or movement will trigger different responses – and of course different audiences respond differently. This is the great tragedy of theatre in these COVID times: the experience depends on intimacy and proximity, sitting huddled in a dark room together with strangers, watching life being projected back at you in a visceral and direct way. In the closed space of a theatre, with work being actively re-created every night, crisis is communicated with real power. There is no substitute for the immediacy.

When constructing a play how do you effectively boil down larger global themes that could otherwise be overwhelming for characters within `their world' so that they can find room to resonate?

I guess it's a bit of a cliché but story has to come from character. Quite often it's one main character, a protagonist who will make things happen through their choices, their desires, their reactions to situations. As many have said before me, always ask, `What is the worst possible thing that could happen to your character?' Then make it happen in your play. That way the character embodies the crisis. It might be an epic crisis, a political crisis or a crisis in a relationship, but we need to see it happen within that character not outside the character. It doesn't happen to someone else, it happens to them – and so whatever vast themes or issues the play is exploring there is an anchor - or multiple anchors in diverse characters.

But this focus on characters should not make us forget the importance of a good story! Personally I come from an Indian storytelling background: my father was very theatrical, he was a singer and he used to tell us long-winded stories and tales with demons and damsels in distress – and he would act them all out. So I have always had a real love of telling stories – characters are tested and revealed through their story and I like characters telling stories that also reflect on them. For me as a writer, every significant character in a play has a story – both a back story (even if it is not revealed) and a journey through the play – and the catalyst for most journeys is some form of crisis. Of course many of my plays deal with very big global themes but I rarely address them directly as that would be too polemical – so I explore them through characters and stories, finding different vantage points and ways of seeing.

What do you feel is the biggest threat to the creation of new drama and plays given the current global crisis? Do we need theatre now more than ever?

From a writer's perspective it's not as bad as it is for most other people who work in theatre. Ultimately we can continue writing, developing new plays, rewriting drafts, getting on with commissions or starting new plays. For the first few weeks I was perhaps too disturbed to write, but since then I have settled and it has been a fertile period for me. However, I do worry whether some of the theatre spaces I know and love will survive and who knows when my new work will find a stage that can produce it. But most of all I really worry for all the freelancers who are almost destitute: stage managers, lighting designers, sound designers, choreographers, directors – you couldn't have a play produced without all of these - and the actors of course – let's not forget the actors –it's very, very difficult. My worry is we're going to lose a lot of talent. People can't live on fresh air. There needs to be a massive new investment in theatre. When urban areas lose the day-time economy of office workers they will need the night-time economy of live performance even more – to bring life and heart back to our towns and cities. When the world is facing multiple crises we need a medium that can help us explore crises in human proportions.

***Lions and Tigers* premiered at the Sam Wanamaker Playhouse, Shakespeare's Globe, London in August 2017**

Based on the true story of her great-uncle and freedom fighter Dinesh Gupta, *Lions and Tigers* is Tanika Gupta's most personal play yet. It charts Dinesh Gupta's emotional and political awakening as this extraordinary nineteen-year-old pits himself against the British Raj.

Scene Four

Tegart *sits astride a chair facing* **Dinesh** *who is led in handcuffed. He remains standing.*

Tegart You look tired, Dinesh.

Dinesh *is silent.*

Tegart Not sleeping too well? Bit close in your cell? Nights are getting warm aren't they?

I need some information, Dinesh. Your court trial is next week and if you cooperate with me it may go easier for you. As it stands, you will hang.

Dinesh I am not afraid to die.

Tegart How's the arm doing?

Dinesh It is healing.

Tegart They got the bullet out.

Dinesh You have good prison doctors.

Tegart Waste of time if you ask me. They should have left the bullets in there so your flesh could rot. Still, it wasn't my call.

Dinesh They want me to look good in court.

Tegart *takes out a piece of paper.*

Tegart You have requested an electric fan, some books, dried mango – a bit of a sweet tooth, eh Dinesh? – a toothbrush and more visiting rights. You've also applied for a new pair of spectacles.

Dinesh My glasses were broken at Writers' Building.

Tegart What do you need to see for? Your eyes will be closed forever very soon.

Dinesh I'd like to see clearly once more before I leave this world.

Tegart If you help me, I will make sure you get your list of things.

Dinesh You are too kind.

Tegart Do you know who I am, Dinesh?

Dinesh Chief of police. Charles Tegart.

Tegart Sir Charles Tegart. How do you know me?

Dinesh There are pictures of you in the papers. I have even seen you in person in disguise at the pickets and demonstrations. You dressed up as a Sikh with a turban last year at the Calcutta congress.

Tegart *looks put out.*

Tegart You're a dupe, Dinesh. One of the many sad rank-and-file young terrorists. You've had your mind poisoned against your natural rulers since your school days. It's no wonder you hate us.

Dinesh It isn't personal.

Tegart Your fanatical leaders are evading arrest whilst you literally take the bullet. They have incited you to murder and brainwashed you. You are a pitiful spectacle. Not even a man yet.

Dinesh I have proved I am a man.

Tegart Probably still a virgin? Not even fucked a woman yet have you?

Perhaps if you had, you wouldn't be so keen to die. All those raging hormones and hot blood, nowhere to go so you channel it all into misguided, dysfunctional patriotism.

Your leaders have played on your weaknesses and your immaturity and saturated you with hatred for the government.

Don't you feel exploited?

Dinesh *does not respond.*

Tegart You Bengalis are not a martial race. You are going against your nature. Books, studies, philosophical debate, natural intelligence, poetry – that's what you Bengalis excel in.

Dinesh So we are the same?

Tegart And how did you come to that conclusion?

Dinesh The Irish – naturally rebellious and poetic – another repressed subject of the British crown and yet here you are serving the empire. You are going against your nature.

Tegart My natural inclination is to serve my king. Earlier this year, two school girls murdered Mr Stevens, the magistrate in Comilla. You were known to be hanging around in Comilla. Did you train those girls?

Dinesh *remains silent.*

Tegart Alright, Mr Gupta, what I need from you are the names of the head of your Jugantar organisation. I know you probably only met them a couple of times because their entire success depends on them remaining shadows. That way they protect themselves.

But you do know who they are. Actually, I have my suspicions but I need more . . . how involved was Subhash Bose in your organisation?

Dinesh *smiles.*

Tegart What are you grinning for?

Dinesh *laughs.*

Tegart What the hell?

Dinesh I never thought I'd get an audience with the chief of police. It's a great honour 'Sir' Tegart.

Tegart The feeling, I assure you, is not mutual.

Dinesh So many young men's lives lost trying to assassinate you. Wasn't there one just a couple of months ago?

Tegart And yet here I sit, alive and well.

I shot the last bastard who tried to kill me. Imagine! Tried to lob a bomb into my car. I sprayed his guts all over the front steps of Writers' Building.

Dinesh He will live again.

Tegart Your oldest brother – a lawyer – isn't he? And your other brother – a doctor. Whilst you – the black sheep of the family . . . bit of a failure.

Your father's contract as the post master in Dhaka has been terminated – lost his job, Dinesh – all because of you.

This is obviously news to **Dinesh** *and he tries hard not to react but he cannot hide his upset.*

Tegart You may well have your deluded martyr's death but your family will suffer.

Dinesh Seven attempts on your life, Sir Tegart.

Tegart Seven?

Dinesh Someone will get you eventually.

Tegart You threatening me?

Dinesh I'm tied up, how could I possibly threaten you?

Tegart No one is going to get me. They've tried, failed and been executed or blown themselves up. I have dodged every single bomb and bullet and I am still very much alive and kicking.

He kicks **Dinesh** *again.*

Tegart But you have forfeited your short life with your cowardly act. Davis was a good man. A loyal servant of the crown. A gentle man. You killed an unarmed man in cold blood.

Dinesh We learn by your example.

Tegart Don't give me that bollocks. Tell me, Dinesh, will your legs shake as you are marched from your cell? Will your bravado desert you as you have to climb those steps? Will you weep like a child and long for your mother's embrace? The noose around your neck, the black hood on your head, your last few gasps with the black hood sucked in and out, through your frightened dried mouth, your young heart racing as you hear the sound of the trap door released with an explosion, the last sound you'll ever hear. The long drop, Dinesh, as you plummet down and then the almighty force of the yanking around your throat, the tightening, burning rope. A broken neck, a few seconds of terrible, agonising, torturous pain, your spinal cord snapped and severed, your lungs exploding, your head splitting unable to scream. For another few seconds you will regret, you will beg God to give you one last miracle. Too late. You will plunge into a bottomless pit of deep, thick, blackness. It will surround and embrace you as you dive into unconsciousness, sinking, sinking, never to swim up to the surface.

Swann *enters and witnesses the scene. He looks but does not say anything.*

Dinesh There are nearly 300 million Indians in this country. One of them will succeed where I failed. You will be killed by our hand. Even a cat has only nine lives.

Tegart What do you mean? Was I the target?

Not Davis?

You were trying to assassinate me? I had an appointment with Davis that morning. Was that why you . . .?

He loses control and punches **Dinesh** *to the floor.*

Tegart Tell me? Was I the target?

Dinesh *smiles.*

Tegart Wipe that fucking evil grin off your face!

He stands on **Dinesh***'s wounded arm.* **Dinesh** *cries out in pain, but* **Tegart** *continues to grind his foot into* **Dinesh***'s shoulder.* **Dinesh** *cries out more.*

Tegart You cowardly, murdering black bastard!

He clocks **Swann** *and steps away.* **Dinesh** *weeps in pain but stares angrily at* **Tegart**.

Tegart Take this miserable, snivelling wretch back to his cell, Chief Superintendent. I am finished with him – for now.

Swann *steps forward and gently helps* **Dinesh** *up. He leads the wounded* **Dinesh** *away.* **Tegart** *looks unnerved.*

A Museum in Baghdad

Hannah Khalil

Hannah Khalil is a playwright and dramatist. Her work for stage includes *A Museum in Baghdad*, which opened at the Royal Shakespeare Company's Swan Theatre in 2019 directed by Erica Whyman; *Interference* at National Theatre of Scotland, *The Scar Test* at Soho Theatre and *Scenes from 68* Years* at the Arcola Theatre. *Scenes from 68* Years* was nominated for the James Tait Black Award and has subsequently been produced by Golden Thread Theatre in San Francisco and in Tunisia (supported by British Council Tunisia and AFAC and produced by Alia Al Zougbi). Her new play Sleepwalking was due to premiere at Hampstead Theatre in April 2020 but was postponed because of the COVID-19 lockdown.

She is currently under commission to write new work for Shakespeare's Globe, Chichester Festival Theatre, The Kiln, Golden Thread in San Francisco and the Central School of Speech and Drama.

Alongside her theatre work, Hannah has written numerous radio plays, including *The Unwelcome*, *Last of the Pearl Fishers* and *The Deportation Room* all for BBC Radio 4. Television work includes multiple episodes of the Channel 4 drama *Hollyoaks*.

What does the word 'crisis' mean to you in a theatrical sense?

The word crisis immediately makes me think about the traditional three-act Aristotelian storytelling model, which is branded like a blunt weapon at young writers and to be frank always scared the hell out of me when I was starting out. The 'moment of crisis' is where in this traditional sense the protagonist has to make a huge decision and the climax follows. I now try to eshew the traditional structure in favour of something tailor-made for each play so that each story finds the form that fits.

How do you feel theatre has the ability to represent/respond to global crises?

If you had asked me this in 2019 I'd have said it has a wonderful ability to react quickly and that that is something that should be avoided at all costs. Because in truth when there are such crises and events it takes time for us to process them. Interestingly, however, throughout the Covid crisis everything I have written, whether it be a short play for children or a full-length play, has ended up on some level reflecting the moment we are in, how I was feeling – the loss of so much. I think really good theatre is about the heart more that the head and it can act as a place for communities to process, and come to terms with what has happened.

Why did you pick this specific scene? What is this scene doing at this point of the play?

I chose this scene because even though the play features two time periods overlapping – 1926 with Gertrude Bell trying to open the museum and 2006 with the Iraqi team trying to reopen post-looting – this is the first time the two moments become one; time bends. And we see the layers of history refracted. It is also the moment that precipitates a moment of crisis for both Gertrude and Ghalia in the play. Gertrude's already waking conscience is pushed even further while Ghalia realises her values do not align with those of her colleagues.

How does this scene speak beyond the wider context of the play?

On the surface this is a beautiful scene of magic realism – but in truth it is about a moment of realisation and understanding. The penny (or coin) really drops for both characters and they understand their place within the power structures of their worlds. The idea and hope is that in watching or reading this scene we will all consider our positions likewise.

As a writer, do you feel a point of crisis is always necessary in a play to create/maintain/sustain drama?

I would never make any rules about what there should or shouldn't be in a play. I think there probably needs to be a climax of some kind – but that can mean anything and can be on a micro if not a macro level.

Does theatre as a form allow for a more effective exploration of crisis in terms of what can be explored, presented and communicated to an audience, in relation to other creative forms?

I think what theatre allows for – in its liveness, its very human liveness – is empathy. As such it has the potential to affect on a visceral level – in my opinion – in a way that solitary art forms do not.

When constructing a play how do you effectively boil down larger global themes that could otherwise be overwhelming for characters within 'their world' so that they can find room to resonate?

It's a truism but 'the personal is political'. How big themes affect normal people is for me the best way to do this. The trick is to do it in an original, theatrical, non-didactic way that catches the audience by surprise and makes them look at something with fresh perspective.

What do you feel is the biggest threat to the creation of new drama and plays given the current global crisis? Do we need theatre now more than ever?

Firstly, of course, the closure of many theatres. I fear making theatre will once again become the domain of the economically privileged few. I also worry that commissioning new writing will be sidelined and an appetite for safe and tried and tested work – and things deemed as pure entertainment will be manufactured by producers who are understandably worried about revenue. Theatre has an important role to play in understanding and grieving what has happened but I fear that because of the economics we will lose a huge amount of theatre makers – not just those starting out but also more established freelancers who were living from job to job – from the industry. Of course 'theatre will survive'. It always has. But many of the incredibly talented friends and colleagues I have made on my journey may have been forced to leave the industry by the time doors are open to audiences again – and the thought of that is heart breaking.

***A Museum in Baghdad* premiered at the RSC's The Other Place, Stratford-upon-Avon in 2019**

In 1926, the nation of Iraq is in its infancy, and British archaeologist Gertrude Bell is founding a museum in Baghdad. In 2006, Ghalia Hussein is attempting to reopen the museum after looting during the war.

Decades apart, these two women share the same goals: to create a fresh sense of unity and nationhood, to make the world anew through the museum and its treasures. One man, the elusive Abu Zaman, caretaker of the museum, watches over the artefacts in both of these unstable times. But questions remain. Who is the museum for? Whose culture are we preserving? And why does it matter when people are dying?

A story of treasured history, desperate choices and the remarkable Gertrude Bell.

Now

Ghalia *enters. She is carrying the box that* **Abu Zaman** *gave to her previously.* **Mohammed** *and* **Abu Zaman** *follow.* **Gertrude** *is writing an article in a corner.*

Ghalia Everyone. Come here. Come on. Who knows about this?

They all look at her in curiosity.

It just appeared – look!

She opens the envelope to reveal the crown from before. It's from the 4,500-year-old royal cemetery at Ur.

York Sweet lord, I've never seen anything like it.

Layla Who from?

Ghalia Abu Zaman?

Abu Zaman *looks blankly at them all.*

Abu Zaman *Melagit.*

Ghalia If 'not found' – then what?

Mohammed All that gold!

York Funny, you'd think someone would steal that – not return it, right?

Layla Maybe they just wanted it off their conscience.

Mohammed It's not exactly common is it – it'd be a nightmare to sell. Maybe whoever took it was just looking after it – keeping it safe.

Layla You can be so naive.

Mohammed That's my youth and optimism for you – attractive isn't it?

Layla *smiles in spite of herself.*

Ghalia When I opened it – it gave me a surge of hope . . . despite all the destruction things can get back to where they belong . . . Isn't it *wonderful*.

Abu Zaman Shall I take it to the basement – lock it up safely there?

York How old is it?

Layla Is it from Ur?

Ghalia Yes – 4,500 years old give or take –

They all stare at it looking beautiful.

Mohammed It's going to look amazing at the opening.

Ghalia What?

Abu Zaman No!

Mohammed We have to find the best way to display it.

York Someone could model it.

Ghalia No, no, it goes under lock and key, it isn't being displayed.

Mohammed This is ridiculous, you are being far too cautious. A museum needs its public or it's just a dead archive.

Ghalia But you *saw* the looting.

Abu Zaman They were possessed, the pounding – thuds, bangs – they broke down the door – a wave – موجةٌ عارمةٌ من الدمار They smashed everything in their way! We need these things intact for the future.

Gertrude / a tidal wave of destruction /

Mohammed No ordinary Iraqis will be at the opening, it's only for dignitaries and journalists.

Ghalia Forget the opening, what about when we lock those flimsy doors at night – who's to say they won't break them down again?

Mohammed You are being paranoid. It has to go on display.

Ghalia No it doesn't.

Mohammed Did you just come back here to lock everything up?

Ghalia Your uncle may be the minister but I'm still the director of the museum and I say *no*.

Mohammed I'm going to call the minister now.

Ghalia I'm right behind you – let's get him on speaker phone. My office. Abu Zaman, come with me, back me up.

Abu Zaman The crown?

Ghalia It has an American soldier guarding it. Come on

The three exit leaving the crown behind them.

Gertrude *steps forward and picks it up.* **Gertrude, Layla** *and* **York** *all look at it. Pause.*

York It's incredible.

Layla Must have belonged to a queen.

Gertrude Beautiful.

York I want to hold it.

Layla You shouldn't touch it without gloves.

York Almost doesn't look real, like a costume.

A beat.

It's a darn shame . . . it was meant to be worn.

Layla By a queen. A goddess.

A beat.

Can you smell –?

Gertrude Burning?

York Why don't you try it on?

Layla Don't be ridiculous.

York Let's get a glimpse of what it would have been like . . . what about it? Don't be a stick-in-the-mud.

Layla My skin could damage it.

York What are you? Bionic woman?

A beat.

It was made to be worn.

A beat.

Come on! It survived the looting – why not? I won't tell.

A beat.

Layla *looks it at.*

York I'll shut the door . . .

Layla *slowly proceeds to take off her head covering, revealing long black hair.* **York** *respectfully turns away.*

Layla It's ok, you can look, you're a woman aren't you?

She unties her hair and it is loose around her shoulders.

York *takes the crown out of* **Gertrude***'s hands. For* **Gertrude** *it vanishes.*

She is looking around for the crown – she can't see it.

Gertrude It's gone!

Layla Come on then, quick.

Gertrude Where?

York *lifts the crown ceremonially.*

Gertrude It belongs here!

York *places the crown on* **Layla***'s head.*

York *steps back to look at her – an in-breath. She looks incredible, regal and beautiful, like a ghost from the past. Her whole demeanour changes – she is transformed.*

At this moment **Gertrude** *sees her too. She places her hand over her mouth in shock at this vision.*

Gertrude The goddess!

Layla I can smell burning . . .

Gertrude SALIM! SALIM! ABU ZAMAN!

Pause.

York *has picked up the camera which is used to log items and held it up to take a photo of* **Layla***. The camera flashes. As soon as this happens* **Gertrude***'s vision vanishes, and she collapses shaking into a chair, her breathing ragged.*

Layla What are you doing?

York I was just taking a picture so you could see.

Layla Put that camera down.

Suddenly **Abu Zaman***,* **Mohammed** *and* **Ghalia** *enter the room.* **Layla** *is affected by the crown – it's as though she's wading through sand.*

Abu Zaman I told you – look – it wasn't safe!

Ghalia What are you doing? Hey!

Layla Be calm.

Ghalia Take it off!

Layla I am.

Mohammed So beautiful.

Ghalia Layla! How can you – be so disrespectful. I'm shocked. What were you thinking?

Layla *takes her hijab and leaves to go to the bathroom and put it back on.*

York It was made to be worn . . .

Abu Zaman It needs to be preserved – to inform future goddesses.

He takes it carefully from her, checks it for damage, wipes it and returns it to its box.

Mohammed Future goddesses? Are you feeling ok, Abu Zaman?

A beat.

York Did you see her – she looked incredible. You should totally display it like that . . . like a statue, a goddess . . . I'm going to help her.

She exits.

Ghalia Unbelievable. If the staff can't be trusted to safeguard the artefacts then what hope is there –

Abu Zaman (*the truth dawning*) What hope is there?

Mohammed Without her hijab she looked . . . amazing (*He catches himself.*) – the crown – looked amazing . . . it was alive.

Ghalia Where are you going?

Mohammed To try and get a mannequin and a wig.

Ghalia What for?

Mohammed To display it.

Ghalia It can't be displayed, I told you it's not safe. What is wrong with you people? Have you lived with the threat of violence for so long you are inured to it?

Mohammed This is a museum – we can make it safe – like my uncle said.

Ghalia None of you listen to me! Is this what I left my family in England for? It's as if you don't care what happens to these things. They belong to the world.

Mohammed Of course I care – but if no one sees them, they may as well not exist.

Emilia

Morgan Lloyd Malcolm

Morgan Lloyd Malcolm is a playwright and screenwriter.

Morgan was commissioned by the Globe to write *Emilia* which became a hit show in summer 2018 before transferring to the West End in 2019. It has been optioned for film and she is currently in development on this as well as several TV drama and comedy projects. She is also developing a book adaptation for film with Lucky Chap Films and adapting her play *The Wasp* into a screenplay for Paradise City Films. She is under commission for stage with Headlong and Clean Break.

Morgan's play *Belongings* was produced at Hampstead Theatre and Trafalgar Studios in 2011 to great acclaim and was shortlisted for the Charles Wintour Most Promising Playwright Award. This was followed in 2015 by another hit play at Hampstead Theatre, *The Wasp*, which also transferred to Trafalgar Studios in 2015.

Other stage work includes commissions for the Old Vic, Clean Break and Firehouse Productions. In 2013 she was chosen as a member of the Soho Six (Soho Theatre). She has co-written several acclaimed immersive site-specific plays with Katie Lyons, produced by Look Left Look Right, including *You Once Said Yes*, *Above and Beyond* and *Once Upon a Christmas*. She was part of the writing team for four of the Lyric Hammersmith's pantomimes from 2009 to 2012 and wrote (solo) the Bolton Octagon's Christmas plays for 2013 and 2014. She has written two large community plays for the Old Vic New Voices: *Platform* and *Epidemic*.

Theatre in Crisis by Morgan Lloyd Malcolm

I feel like when we reach a crisis point we shed our masks. We lose our filters. We cut the crap. We say the things that have been bubbling inside us for so long waiting for the right opportunity to escape our mouths. Writing this play felt like this. Performing this play felt like this. And for Emilia2 it's like a dam is bursting in this moment.

I feel very much like what is happening currently with the pandemic and everything that has been going on in 2020 we are at a crisis point where the filters are being shed. People are speaking plainly. Demands are being made. Changes need to happen. In fact whole structures need to be broken down. Emilia2, in this moment, is awakening. It feels very similar to what we're going through now.

We need stories and theatre and art to process what is happening to us. To help us understand what we can do to heal and repair. And to ask important questions about what can be different. What can be better. It's in our art that we dream and we imagine a better world for everyone. Just like Emilia2 in this scene I feel like we are waking up at the moment. And when we do the dreams we weave should inform how we rebuild our societies for the better.

In this scene Emilia2 has just transformed from Emilia1. The catalyst for the transformation is the death of her baby daughter and it comes off the back of a series of events that have beaten her down from her previously strong, hopeful, youthful self. It is a true crisis point. She has reached the end of her ability to maintain her usual composure. She cannot keep up the facade of being okay with her situation. And most importantly she's had enough of Shakespeare who she is talking to in this speech.

***Emilia* premiered at Shakespeare's Globe, London, in 2018**

In 1611 Emilia Bassano penned a volume of radical, feminist and subversive poetry. It was one of the first published collections of poetry written by a woman in England. The little we know of Emilia Bassano is restricted to the possibility that she may have been the 'Dark Lady' of Shakespeare's sonnets – and the rest of HerStory has been erased by History.

Originally commissioned for Shakespeare's Globe, and with an all-female cast, this ground-breaking play reveals the life of Emilia: poet, mother and feminist. This time, the focus is on this exceptional woman who managed to outlive all the men the history books tethered her to.

Act 1 Scene 9

Shakespeare *enters.*

Shakespeare I heard. Are you alright?

Emilia2 No.

Shakespeare What can I do?

Emilia2 Nothing.

Shakespeare Nothing will come of nothing.

Emilia2 I cannot heave my heart into my mouth. There are no words for what I am feeling.

Shakespeare I know my love.

Emilia2 Do you?

Shakespeare You know I do.

Emilia2 And yet you find them. Again and again. The pain and anguish of your own losses written large upon the stage. Does it help? I think it must. If only my own grief could be dissipated as such. But it can't. Can it? And it is because of this that grief is not my only pain. It is my whole existence in your shadow. It is women born to a status that dooms us to your ill will. That there be women that do abuse their husbands I am of no doubt but the balance is grossly tipped in your favour. That we must assume that everything we do is to be dismissed. That all talent and interest, all passion and sense is just a quirk of our sex that can be indulged but never validated. That we must instead sit quietly and patiently watch as you enjoy the fruits of your labours. Imagine it so for you. Then see how my own desires languish in the dark. And still your sex think we are less? That we have less, to be able to survive? That somehow perhaps we feel less? Well, I would that you use your privileged position in that wooden O of words to let husbands know, their wives have sense like them. They see and smell and have their palates, both for sweet and sour, as husbands have. What is it that they do when they change us for others? Is it sport? I think it is. And does affection breed it? I think it does. Is it frailty that thus errs? It is so too. And have not we affections. Desires for sport, and frailty, as men have? Then let them use us well; else let them know, the ills we do, their ills instruct us so. Get out.

Shakespeare Emilia, you are full of grief. Stop.

Emilia2 Get out!

Shakespeare I will return when you are at peace.

Emilia2 I will never be at peace as long as I have no voice!

Shakespeare *leaves.*

Emilia2 I will not stop. I will not rest until I find words for my Odilya. And for all my daughters I will never know.

X

Alistair McDowall

Alistair McDowall grew up in the North East of England. Plays include: *The Glow* (Royal Court Theatre TBC); *all of it* (Royal Court Theatre 2020); *Zero for the Young Dudes!* (National Theatre Connections 2017); *X* (Royal Court Theatre 2016); *Pomona* (RWCMD/Gate Theatre 2014; Orange Tree Theatre/Royal Exchange Theatre/National Theatre 2014/15); *Talk Show* (Royal Court Theatre 2013); *Brilliant Adventures* (Royal Court Young Writers' Festival 2012; Royal Exchange, Manchester and Live Theatre, Newcastle 2013); and *Captain Amazing* (Live Theatre, Newcastle and Edinburgh Fringe 2013; UK tour 2014). He is a MacDowell fellow, and a recipient of the Harold Pinter Commission. His work has been translated and produced internationally.

Theatre in Crisis by Alistair McDowall

In my work normally, if I'm thinking of the word 'crisis,' it's usually a crisis of confidence on my own part. What if this is terrible? What if this play is so terrible it closes the theatre and I'm run out of town by an angry mob?

Those worries all seem comically small now that the problem is gathering people in a theatre to watch a play would be literally life-threatening.

Aside from the conversations about how to save the industry, how to make work, there've also been lots of conversations about how to respond to this crisis in our work.

I've never been the kind of writer able to look at a global event or a wider political issue and build my play around that – whenever I've tried, the play has fallen to pieces before it's even got going. Instead, I have to focus all my care and attention on the characters and their immediate circumstances – what do they want, and how are they going to get it? That's not to say my plays aren't political – I think all of them are. It's just that I trust that if my characters are as well-rounded and human as I can make them, then the wider world will seep into their bones just as it has into mine.

Their anger and desire for change will boil up within the action of the play whether I want it to or not.

I've also felt recently that I can engage with the world just as effectively through the form and structure of my plays as I can through the characters and what they have to say for themselves – that's part of the reason why I chose this particular scene.

This scene from my play *X* seemed the most extreme 'crisis' I could find in any of my work – a complete breakdown of memory and language; a dissolving of the self. Everything in the play has been building to this moment – it's when the façade hiding the chaos roiling beneath is torn away, and everything falls apart. Everything after this scene is a rebuilding – an attempt to find a new way of living.

I also think it's the best way I can illustrate how I feel theatre is often most effective when attacking ideas through metaphor. I wanted to write a play about losing someone you loved with every atom of your being – I didn't think I could get anywhere close to that through direct conversation within the play. Instead, I sent the characters to Pluto and began dismantling the play around them, pulling at the loose threads keeping their reality together. To me this seemed the fastest route to get to the heart of that pain.

I've been thinking about this approach more throughout this strange time – I think it'd be a mistake for me to try and write 'a Covid play' – aside from the fact I wouldn't know where to start, I also think the last thing people are going to want to hear about after living through a pandemic is what it was like living through a pandemic.

But the more universal, lasting impact of this time on our psychology, how we live, how we interact with each other, how we value (or didn't value enough) community and physical contact with each other – those things seem to me very fertile ground for theatre to explore; for theatremakers to find new forms and structures for our stories that reflect the new form and structure our lives have taken on. The act of bringing an audience together to watch a play is going to feel like such a monumental thing when it happens again – if I was part of that audience I'd want to laugh and cry and feel. I'd want to see work that resonated with how this crisis has felt rather than work just intent on telling me what it was.

I'd also like to see as much work as possible by people with lives different to my own. I'd like to be reminded that my community is bigger than just the people living in my house. The film critic Roger Ebert used to call cinema the 'empathy machine' which I always thought was a more accurate label for theatre – we gather together to watch ourselves in the flesh. We walk a few miles in the shoes of people we can see fighting and yearning and pushing and pulling right in front of us.

Recently it's become clear how essential it is to listen to each other's stories – to really listen.

Closing ourselves off from our wider community enables diseases like racism to fester.

The theatre should be a place where people from all backgrounds are given space to speak and tell their stories. A house of listening.

It hasn't always taken on that responsibility.

I hope when it returns it will. We will.

I hope when we can all gather together again, we do so to listen to each other.

_X_ premiered at the Royal Court Theatre, London in 2016

Billions of miles from home, the lone research base on Pluto has lost contact with Earth. After their clocks glitch and fail, all sense of how long they've been trapped there is lost.

Acting Captain Gilda claims she's seen a young woman arrive and enter the base.

After the others find no evidence of this, order begins to break down and chaos takes hold.

Just prior to this scene, another crew member has died, leaving Gilda and Clark attempting to cling onto their memories and sense of self as their minds reach breaking point.

Clark . . . Is he in the freezer now.

Gilda Yes, but don't . . .

Don't think about that.

Pause.

Clark How long do you think it was?

Gilda . . . I don't know.

Clark . . . Do you –

Do you think it was months, or *years* –

Gilda I don't know.

Pause.

Clark He just lay there the whole time, and we couldn't even –

Gilda We did the best we could.

. . .

We couldn't –

. . .

We did what we could.

Pause.

Clark He was a good captain.

Pause.

Gilda He was/n't –

Clark He was the –

Gilda He wasn't the captain.

. . .

He was a meteorologist.

Clark . . .

Gilda He was a scientist. Like me.

Clark . . . Yeah.

. . .

. . .

That's what I – I meant.

. . .

Pause.

Gilda Are you alright?

Pause.

Clark I don't know.

. . .

. . .

I can't . . .

. . .

I really feel like I'm hanging on by my nails here –

How long have you been standing there?

Gilda You're okay –

Clark I can't even tell if –

Gilda We'll do it together.

Clark . . .

Gilda We can help each other.

Clark . . .

Gilda Okay?

. . .

Start again.

Clark I don't get it.

Gilda Start again.

Clark I don't get what you mean –

Gilda Start again.

Clark I told you –

Gilda Tell it again. Tell me.

Pause.

Gilda You're in here.

Pause.

Clark I'm in here. It's – I'm sitting –

. . .

. . .

I see her at the window.

Gilda What's she look like?

Clark Like a – Person.

Gilda Small –

Clark Like a person looks.

Gilda Is she smiling?

Clark I can't see because of the – Reflection –

Gilda Then she disappears.

Clark She comes in –

Gilda You let her in.

Clark No, I – She –

Gilda She gets in here,

Clark I back away –

Gilda You're scared.

Clark I back away and fall,

Gilda And you're in here.

Pause.

Clark No.

Gilda No?

Clark No, that's not – That wasn't –

That wasn't mine.

Pause.

Gilda How about –

Clark Start again.

Gilda I have a ball.

Clark A ball.

Gilda I have a ball and you're working.

Clark I'm doing maths.

Gilda I'm bored.

Clark I need –

Gilda I don't like things that aren't real.

Clark I'm limping.

Gilda You're limping.

Clark My name is . . .

Gilda X

Clark I'm . . .

. . .

No.

Gilda Maths is for –

Clark No it's, this isn't –

Gilda I get further away.

Clark She gets further away.

Gilda I have a son

Clark Daughter

Gilda Who is . . .

Clark X

Gilda years

Clark Further away

Gilda To always make me tell

Clark X

Gilda For *years*

Clark leaving

Gilda You need a

Clark Computer science.

Gilda Calculator

Clark Left

Gilda X

Clark X

Pause.

Clark Carrr . . .

Gilda Carl –

Clark C – Cl-Cllarr –

Gilda X

Clark X

Gilda Co –

Clark Coa –

Gilda Coast –

Clark Coarse –

Gilda Claw –

Clark Claws –

Gilda X

Clark X

Gilda And the algorithm –

Clark Watch

Gilda Rain

Clark Rain

Gilda Rail

Clark X

Gilda And

– I'm in here

– It's

– I'm

– X

– at the window

– See

– X

– at the

– X

– at

– the girls

– she

– nothing

– my mother

– left

– *No.*

– X

– No.

– . . .

– . . .

– Start again –

– I'm in

– She

– X

– and

– all the –

– X

– X

– hear

– X

– not

– Where

– X

– Enough to

– lift

– X

– Punch the

– X

– crowd

– X

– X

– X

– X

– She

– South America

– South America

– South Amer

– South America

– she's

– X

– One the last

– pillarwebs

– Two

– She's

– X

– One in the freezer

– X in the freezer

– *Two* in the freezer –

– Two in the South Amer

– X

– in the fr

– X

– And

– And

– Birds

– Bird

– Birds

– X

– brush

– brushing

– brush against the

– X

– X

– X

– . . .

– . . .

– Glll –

– Glarr –

– X

– Luscin –

– Glllaah –

– Luscina –

– X

– Lus –

– Glll –

– G –

– G –

– da

– daaaaa

– X

– X

– X / X X X X X X X

– X X X X X X X X / X X X

– Everything

– X

– hold onto X

– hold onto / X in particu X she

– X X X X

– X X X X X X / X X X X X X X X X X X X X X X X

– X X X X X X X X X X X X X X X X / X X X X

– X X X X X / X X X X X X X X X X X X / X

– X

–X/X

–X

–X

XXXXXXXXXXXXXXXXXXXXXXXXXXXXXXX
XXXXXXXXXXXXXXXXXXXXXXXXXXXXXXX
XXXXXXXXXXXXXXXXXXXXXXXXXXXXXXX
XXXXXXXXXXXXXXXXXXXXXXXXXXXXXXX
XXXXXXXXXXXXXXXXXXXXXXXXXXXXXXX
XXXXXXXXXXXXXXXXXXXXXXXXXXXXXXX
XXXXXXXXXXXXXXXXXXXXXXXXXXXXXXX
XXXXXXXXXXXXXXXXXXXXXXXXXXXXXXX
XXXXXXXXXXXXXXXXXXXXXXXXXXXXXXX
XXXXXXXXXXXXXXXXXXXXXXXXXXXXXXX
XXXXXXXXXXXXXXXXXXXXXXXXXXXXXXX
XXXXXXXXXXXXXXXXXXXXXXXXXXXXXXX
XXXXXXXXXXXXXXXXXXXXXXXXXXXXXXX
XXXXXXXXXXXXXXXXXXXXXXXXXXXXXXX
XXXXXXXXXXXXXXXXXXXXXXXXXXXXXXX
XXXXXXXXXXXXXXXXXXXXXXXXXXXXXXX
XXXXXXXXXXXXXXXXXXXXXXXXXXXXXXX
XXXXXXXXXXXXXXXXXXXXXXXXXXXXXXX
XXXXXXXXXXXXXXXXXXXXXXXXXXXXXXX
XXXXXXXXXXXXXXXXXXXXXXXXXXXXXXX
XXXXXXXXXXXXXXXXXXXXXXXXXXXXXXX
XXXXXXXXXXXXXXXXXXXXXXXXXXXXXXX
XXXXXXXXXXXXXXXXXXXXXXXXXXXXXXX
XXXXXXXXXXXXXXXXXXXXXXXXXXXXXXX

xXXXXXXXXXXXXXXXXXXXXXXXXXXXXXX

xXXXXXXXXXXXXXXXXXXXXXXXXXXXXXX

xXXXXXXXXXXXXXXXXXXXXXXXXXXXXXX

xXXXXXXXXXXXXXXXXXXXXXXXXXXXXXX

xXXXXXXXXXXXXXXXXXXXXXXXXXXXXXX

xXXXXXXXXXXXXXXXXXXXXXXXXXXXXXX

xXXXXXXXXXXXXXXXXXXXXXXXXXXXXXX

xXXXXXXXXXXXXXXXXXXXXXXXXXXXXXX

xXXXXXXXXXXXXXXXXXXXXXXXXXXXXXX

xXXXXXXXXXXXXXXXXXXXXXXXXXXXXXX

xXXXXXXXXXXXXXXXXXXXXXXXXXXXXXX

xXXXXXXXXXXXXXXXXXXXXXXXXXXXXXX

xXXXXXXXXXXXXXXXXXXXXXXXXXXXXXX

xXXXXXXXXXXXXXXXXXXXXXXXXXXXXXX

xXXXXXXXXXXXXXXXXXXXXXXXXXXXXXX

xXXXXXXXXXXXXXXXXXXXXXXXXXXXXXX

xXXXXXXXXXXXXXXXXXXXXXXXXXXXXXX

xXXXXXXXXXXXXXXXXXXXXXXXXXXXXXX

xXXXXXXXXXXXXXXXXXXXXXXXXXXXXXX

xXXXXXXXXXXXXXXXXXXXXXXXXXXXXXX

xXXXXXXXXXXXXXXXXXXXXXXXXXXXXXX

xXXXXXXXXXXXXXXXXXXXXXXXXXXXXXX

xXXXXXXXXXXXXXXXXXXXXXXXXXXXXXX

xXXXXXXXXXXXXXXXXXXXXXXXXXXXXXX

xXXXXXXXXXXXXXXXXXXXXXXXXXXXXXX

xXXXXXXXXXXXXXXXXXXXXXXXXXXXXXX

xXXXXXXXXXXXXXXXXXXXXXXXXXXXXXX

XXXXXXXXXXXXXXXXXXXXXXXXXXXXXXX
XXXXXXXXXXXXXXXXXXXXXXXXXXXXXXX
XXXXXXXXXXXXXXXXXXXXXXXXXXXXXXX
XXXXXXXXXXXXXXXXXXXXXXXXXXXXXXX
XXXXXXXXXXXXXXXXXXXXXXXXXXXXXXX
XXXXXXXXXXXXXXXXXXXXXXXXXXXXXXX
XXXXXXXXXXXXXXXXXXXXXXXXXXXXXXX
XXXXXXXXXXXXXXXXXXXXXXXXXXXXXXX
XXXXXXXXXXXXXXXXXXXXXXXXXXXXXXX
XXXXXXXXXXXXXXXXXXXXXXXXXXXXXXX
XXXXXXXXXXXXXXXXXXXXXXXXXXXXXXX
XXXXXXXXXXXXXXXXXXXXXXXXXXXXXXX
XXXXXXXXXXXXXXXXXXXXXXXXXXXXXXX
XXXXXXXXXXXXXXXXXXXXXXXXXXXXXXX
XXXXXXXXXXXXXXXXXXXXXXXXXXXXXXX
XXXXXXXXXXXXXXXXXXXXXXXXXXXXXXX
XXXXXXXXXXXXXXXXXXXXXXXXXXXXXXX
XXXXXXXXXXXXXXXXXXXXXXXXXXXXXXX
XXXXXXXXXXXXXXXXXXXXXXXXXXXXXXX
XXXXXXXXXXXXXXXXXXXXXXXXXXXXXXX
XXXXXXXXXXXXXXXXXXXXXXXXXXXXXXX
XXXXXXXXXXXXXXXXXXXXXXXXXXXXXXX
XXXXXXXXXXXXXXXXXXXXXXXXXXXXXXX
XXXXXXXXXXXXXXXXXXXXXXXXXXXXXXX
XXXXXXXXXXXXXXXXXXXXXXXXXXXXXXX
XXXXXXXXXXXXXXXXXXXXXXXXXXXXXXX
XXXXXXXXXXXXXXXXXXXXXXXXXXXXXXX

An Adventure

Vinay Patel

Vinay Patel's debut play, *True Brits*, opened at the Edinburgh Fringe 2014, before transferring to the Bush Theatre and Vault Festival. His latest play, *An Adventure*, ran at the Bush Theatre in late 2018. His first piece for television, *Murdered by My Father*, won the Royal Television Society Award for Best Single Drama and was nominated for three BAFTAs. He was named a BAFTA Breakthrough Brit for his work.

Vinay has since written for Paines Plough, ITV, Channel 4 and the BFI, as well as contributing to the bestselling collection of essays *The Good Immigrant*. Most recently, he wrote for the eleventh and twelfth series of *Doctor Who* – receiving a Hugo nomination – and is developing further projects for TV, theatre and film.

What does the word 'crisis' mean to you in a theatrical sense?

A dramatic play will likely contain lots of difficult choices for your characters, but for me the moment of crisis involves the choice that most fully tests your protagonist once you've established all the parameters of their situation and desires. They say that drama is picking between two bad choices, and you can't find the most effective point of crisis for your characters until we understand what bad is for them.

How do you feel theatre has the ability to represent/respond to global crises?

I think modern media has shifted the role that we require from drama and theatre in particular. It feels to me that there's less a need for the simpler styles of reportage, journalistic theatre that want to 'show' you a thing that's happening. Other mediums are faster and more information-rich in that regard. However, theatre allows the filtering of that deluge of information into *emotionally* rich perspectives that lets us slow things down and consider those perspectives together. So rarely now are we all experiencing the same thing so those moments that we do matter more than they did.

Why did you pick this specific scene? What is this scene doing at this point of the play?

I picked this scene because watching the actors perform it broke my heart every night. It's two humans, Jyoti and Rasik, who started off their marriage in good faith and with mutual ambition for more, now finding their concepts of 'more' clashing irreconcilably.

Rasik is not a terrible person, exactly. He truly thinks he's learned from their previous arguments and is doing the right thing by his wife and family. It still comes from the same energy that drew them together in the first place. But while he might be able to see that he's let her down and wants to do better, he still can't understand how much he's truly asking of Jyoti or really see the woman she's become.

How does this scene speak beyond the wider context of the play?

The dilemma here is one I think will be familiar to many people: How do you best serve your family? How long can one keep up a broader struggle if it'll impact on the well-being of those you love most? And how the people who tend to rein in their ambitions for the sake of others tend to be women.

As a writer, do you feel a point of crisis is always necessary in a play to create/maintain/sustain drama?

I don't know if it's necessary, exactly – a play can be compelling to me as long as it knows what it's doing and why it's doing it. You can be pulled along by the force of a vision. But drama lives in the churn, the movement, the response, the change, and you can't get those things without your character making the decisions that generate them.

Does theatre as a form allow for a more effective exploration of crisis in terms of what can be explored, presented and communicated to an audience, in relation to other creative forms?

Well, theatre (or at least classically dramatic theatre) is in some sense a behavioural study. How and why do we act in certain ways when presented with an obstacle? It allows us to inhabit surrogates that push us to consider how we might also act in that situation. While other forms can do that too of course, personally I find it easier to place my empathy when there's a real person in front of me.

When constructing a play how do you effectively boil down larger global themes that could otherwise be overwhelming for characters within 'their world' so that they can find room to resonate?

In the main I think it's about finding perspectives on those larger themes and having your characters embody those perspectives. The trick is to create a counter-spin for those characters as well so they're surprising and unexpected and truthful, not just a mouthpiece. Then it's about whether the drama of the play is set up in such a way as to challenge those perspectives.

What do you feel is the biggest threat to the creation of new drama and plays given the current global crisis? Do we need theatre now more than ever?

I mean. Money. Always. Not just in the payment of artists from their works but also the means of people being able to just survive. You'll likely need another job if you want to be a playwright and right now, for so many people, those jobs are either being limited or disappearing entirely. That means less time to write, and more pressures elsewhere in your life. The upshot is I fear we will undo a lot of the good work theatres have been doing to be more inclusive – in every sense – and end up with a medium that feels like a luxury because it can only be made by people who have the capacity to treat it as such.

***An Adventure* premiered at the Bush Theatre, London in September 2018**

On a stormy night in 1954, a woman doomed to marry one of five men discovers the wildcard choice might just be the person she'd been hoping for all along. *An Adventure* follows headstrong Jyoti and her fumbling suitor Rasik as they ride the crest of the fall of the British Empire from the shores of post-partition India to the forests of Mau Mau Kenya onto the industrial upheaval of 1970s London and the present day.

But what happens when youthful ambitions crash hard against reality? When you look back at the story of your time together, can you bear to ask yourself: was it all worth it?

Witty, charming and full of fearless historical insight, *An Adventure* is an epic, technicolour love story from one of the country's most promising young writers about the people who journeyed to British shores in hope and shaped the country we live in today.

5. London, England

Jyoti *in a sari and workman's jacket. She shivers as she clutches a tattered placard. It's freezing. Raining hard.*

Rasik *enters, fully suited. A newspaper covering his head from the rain.*

Rasik (*speaking loudly over the rain*) You're on your own?

Jyoti The others are coming.

Rasik That doesn't look fun.

Jyoti It's a hunger strike, it's not meant to be fun!

Rasik Oh. So I better toss this away then.

He holds up a container.

Jyoti What's that?

Rasik Sandwich. Your favourite. Lashings of mustard and mayonnaise.

Jyoti *looks at the container, longingly.*

Jyoti Get under here, it's dry.

Rasik *joins her, they huddle close together. He hands her the container, points behind her. Speaking normally now.*

Rasik Do they even know you're out here?

Jyoti They know. And if they think they can get away with just withdrawing their support (*shouting, to the building behind*) they can think again!

Rasik You're picketing the union, for your union . . . because they won't let you be a union anymore. Look at you. My little Gandhi!

Jyoti If you've come here to mock me, go do it with your work pals instead.

Rasik No I'm sorry, I didn't mean – I'm sorry.

So is it true? That they've suspended all your memberships?

A beat.

I'm here to listen, I promise.

Jyoti They said they don't like our tactics.

Rasik I see.

Jyoti Too aggressive, 'damaging an already imperilled Labour government' blah blah blah.

Rasik Guess solidarity only goes so far. Proves it though. That their support isn't worth much. Proves that there's no reason for you to be out here.

She looks at him, suspicious.

Jyoti You're not here to bring me a sandwich, are you, Rasik?

Rasik Man can't bring his hungry wife a sandwich?

Jyoti You've never made me a sandwich in your life. Come on. Out with it.

A beat.

Rasik You've done your part. It's someone else's turn to step up.

Jyoti Like who?

A beat.

Rasik Like me.

He beams, willing her to guess. **Jyoti** *slowly clocks what's happened.*

Jyoti A promotion?

Rasik Not just any promotion. *The* promotion. Head of my own surveying team. Build the reputation, build the contacts then go private sector in a couple of years. Only way from here is up, up, up! Now, I'm going to say a number. Fifteen hundred.

Jyoti Fifteen hundred what?

Rasik Pounds. Fifteen hundred pounds. That's what they gave me, a bonus.

A beat.

What's that face for?

Jyoti Nothing I –

I thought there'd be more time.

Rasik More time? We've been here nearly twenty years, Jyoti!

Jyoti I know, I know . . .

Rasik This is your success too. You've earned it.

You know that house? The one on the corner of the park? That you point out every time we go past?

Jyoti Reminds me of home.

Rasik Well, we're getting that house. I've put the bonus down as a deposit . . .

Jyoti You what?

Rasik . . . and by next month we'll have gotten out of that heap we've been stuck in, that makes us hate each other, to somewhere bigger. Nicer. Warmer! Somewhere the girls can be *proud* to come home to, with their own families some day. You could use those genius hands of yours to build our own little kingdom, leave all this behind and –

Jyoti You mean leave my job.

Rasik I said leave all this behind.

Though if you want to talk about the job . . . it's kind of already left you.

A beat as he realises that's too sharp, then tries to pivot to the positives.

But that doesn't matter, you don't need it anymore. Hey, we could even take a holiday. Imagine us, little old us, thirty thousand feet above the sea, going somewhere because we *want* to, not because we *have* to!

Jyoti How did you get the money?

Rasik Sorry?

Jyoti The 'bonus'. They don't just hand those out. What did you do?

Rasik Well. I proved myself.

A pause.

Jyoti You broke your strike.

A beat.

You're a scab?! I can't believe –

Rasik Don't call me that!

It was my chance! I never had a break, you know I never had one and then, there it was, a chance to shove it in the face of all those bastards, Tompkins, Barker, OWENS!

Bloody Owens! He thinks nothing of you or me, why should I have solidarity with him? He doesn't deserve it! They never really had it with us, so when I have a chance to show that I *care*, I care for that company when all they do is sit around and . . .

He finally acknowledges **Jyoti***'s silence.*

Jyoti I feel like. You're laughing at me. You've come here to laugh at me.

Rasik No no, I know your ladies are decent people, our people, *they* deserve better, but these guys? Jesus, they –

Please. Please don't look at me like that.

Jyoti Do you think what I'm doing is a joke?

A beat.

Rasik Not for *you* . . .

Jyoti Wow. Ok. Can you . . .

Rasik Jyoti –

Jyoti I need you to leave?

Go. Please. Let me think for a second, please let me think for a . . .

Rasik *pulls out an envelope from his jacket pocket.*

Jyoti What's that?

Rasik Her acceptance letter.

Jyoti Sonal? Where?

Rasik To Newcastle. She's going to Newcastle. I promised her she could go, and it's time I started living up to my promises. And not just to her, anything we want can happen, Sonal has her studies, you can stay at home, help Roshni with school, you're so smart . . .

Jyoti Rasik –

Rasik . . . smarter than me –

Jyoti I don't think that's what I –

Rasik Hey, hey . . . Listen. Listen to me.

A desperation in his voice here.

I realised something the other week. I was out having a drink, buttering up one of the clients, and he said he was surprised that he still loved his wife after all these years and I realised that I've never said that to you. That's mad, isn't it? How we've never said that. I've never made you feel like you deserve, how your father would've wanted, what your mother would've wished for, I've not delivered *you* what I promised either but . . .

I love you, Jyoti.

You're my guide, my hero, my north star, you –

Jyoti Stop.

Please. Stop. Stop giving me the sell, I'm too tired for the sell.

You don't need to butter me up. I get the idea. I get what you want.

They stare at each other. Neither of them quite sure what they're feeling.

Rasik This could be our lives just beginning, if you'll let it. So will you let it?

Jyoti *looks at the container. Back up to* **Rasik**.

The Effect

Lucy Prebble

Lucy Prebble is a writer for film, television, games and theatre.

Lucy is co-executive producer and writer on the BAFTA, Golden Globe and Emmy award-winning HBO drama *Succession*, for which she has also won a WGA Award.

For television, she has written *I Hate Suzie* which was co-created with her close friend Billie Piper for Sky Atlantic and aired in 2020. She is the creator of the TV series *Secret Diary of a Call Girl* (ITV/Showtime), and has recently made a pilot for HBO starring Sarah Silverman. Lucy also writes for Frankie Boyle's *New World Order* (BBC) and appears on the TV show as a guest as well as appearing regularly on *Have I Got News for You*.

For theatre, Lucy has written the political and emotional meta-thriller *A Very Expensive Poison* which was a huge five-star hit for the Old Vic in 2019 and Olivier nominated for Best New Play, It won the Critics' Circle Award for Best New Play and Best New Production of a Play at the Broadway World Awards.

Before that, *The Effect*, a study of love and neuroscience, was performed at the National Theatre and also won the Critics' Circle Award for Best New Play.

Lucy also wrote *Enron*, a hugely successful piece about the infamous corporate fraud, which transferred to the West End and Broadway after sell-out runs at both the Royal Court and Chichester Festival Theatre. Her first play, *The Sugar Syndrome* (2003), won her the George Devine Award and was performed at the Royal Court.

Lucy is the recipient of the 2019 Wellcome Screenwriting Fellowship, allowing her to explore where the world of film meets science and research.

Lucy also writes video games and is fascinated by new technology and storytelling. She contributes to major publications as a journalist and wrote a weekly tech column for the *Observer* newspaper. In games, she was head scene writer for Bungie's massively successful first-person shooter video game *Destiny*.

What does the word 'crisis' mean to you in a theatrical sense?

I suppose I think about times in life, or in a play, where there is no escape. Where someone can't hide anymore. Where all defence mechanisms are applied and rendered useless. Where character, in life and in fiction, is revealed.

How do you feel theatre has the ability to represent/respond to global crises?

Pretty well, it's been something I've tried to do throughout my career. Theatre can happen more quickly and more cheaply than other art forms and where there is less money, there are fewer lawsuits too.

Why did you pick this specific scene? What is this scene doing at this point of the play?

It's a mirror scene to a seduction scene earlier in the play, where the two volunteers on a trial fall in love. This is the mirror scene, a terrible fight when they are being given powerful drugs. It's a scene where one is withholding something from the other and that love splinters. It's a crisis in trust, health and understanding.

As a writer, do you feel a point of crisis is always necessary in a play to create/maintain/sustain drama?

I'm not conscious of that, but it probably should be.

Does theatre as a form allow for a more effective exploration of crisis in terms of what can be explored, presented and communicated to an audience, in relation to other creative forms?

Umm. I'm not sure. I think a lot of writing for theatre makes use of dramatic irony, which is the technique whereby the audience know something that one or more characters on stage doesn't know, and this is often used to create tension, up to the point where the secret is out, or Chekhov's gun is fired. That sense of crisis being both avertable and also inevitable is very common in theatre stories and is probably reflecting something profound about life. I'm not sure what.

When constructing a play how do you effectively boil down larger global themes that could otherwise be overwhelming for characters within 'their world' so that they can find room to resonate?

I don't really do this. I just think about feelings and thoughts and voices within me, of which there are many, and then I examine and amplify them in dramatic ways. We all have whole casts within us. Rarely do I boil theme down to character. Theme is used to inform world and often form, but not character.

What do you feel is the biggest threat to the creation of new drama and plays given the current global crisis? Do we need theatre now more than ever?

It's a dangerous time. I think people feel disturbed already by lack of congregation. I think there is a danger of a whole generation losing heart when it was a tough enough art form to exist in to begin with. It is heartbreaking and short-sighted that there isn't a bailout considered for the industry in the way that financial industries get rescued as a matter of course. That sends a sad message to society. Your lives are dependent on banks. Your economy is more important than your lives. Your art is a luxury, and a sacrifice made willingly. There was nothing we could do. There was nothing we could do.

The Effect premiered at the National Theatre's Cottesloe Theatre, London in November 2012

The Effect is a clinical romance. Two young volunteers, Tristan and Connie, agree to take part in a clinical drug trial. Succumbing to the gravitational pull of attraction and love, however, Tristan and Connie manage to throw the trial off-course, much to the frustration of the clinicians involved. This funny, moving and perhaps surprisingly human play explores questions of sanity, neurology and the limits of medicine, alongside ideas of fate, loyalty and the inevitability of physical attraction.

Tristan I love you. I'm sick with missing you.

He kisses her. She pulls away.

Connie No.

Tristan What?

Connie I want it to be fair.

Tristan Fair? What?! Is this about him? Have you talked to him?

Connie I'm just trying to keep this safe.

Tristan Safe? Are you frightened of me now?

Connie No. Should I be?

Tristan Yeah I'm a fucking monster. Just say what you mean.

Connie I am. I'm saying no.

Tristan To what?

Connie I'm in a relationship and you're clearly not a relationship kind of guy –

Tristan Where did that come from?!

Connie You're a flirty, you know, bit of a player type –

Tristan No I'm not!

Connie I've seen you flirt with the doctor for God's sake.

Tristan Are you joking? Christ, Connie, she's nearly fifty!

Connie Yeah, are you saying women can't be attractive in their forties?!

Tristan What, I'm the one that's been flirting with her apparently! . . . Has she been saying things about me?

Connie It's none of your business.

Tristan You're not telling me something.

Connie You're being weird.

Tristan You're lying.

Connie I haven't said anything, how can I be lying?!

Tristan By not telling me stuff.

Connie There's loads of stuff I'm not telling you all the time, otherwise it would be unbearable!

Tristan That's exactly the sort of thing people say when they're lying.

She runs her hands through her hair in stress. Her hair comes out in her hands.

Connie My hair's coming out.

Tristan Mine's coming out too.

Connie Yeah but not because of the drug.

Tristan Fuck you.

Connie I didn't mean that!

Tristan Just don't rewrite what's happened. Don't make out / I'm –

Connie / I'm not! What do you care anyway? That's in the past. I thought you wanted to live *now*?

Tristan I want *you* to live *now*. You're always talking about what happens afterwards or how we got here, tell me what you feel *now*?

Connie It doesn't matter what I feel, what does it matter –

Tristan / Because I'm asking you!

Connie I don't know!

Tristan You're so scared. Why are you so scared all the time?! It's like being with an old woman. What might go wrong though?

Connie This is my life!

Tristan Exactly!

Connie You don't care do you?

Tristan Course I do.

Connie Because you just want it NOW. You know maybe you *should* start thinking about the future a bit.

Tristan What?!

Connie This isn't exactly a gap year, Tris. It's become a sort of gap life.

Tristan That's a terrible thing to say to me.

Connie Then don't say I'm boring just cos I'm not giving you what you want!

Tristan Are you saying I'm not good enough for you?

Connie No I'm saying sort your*self* out / –

Tristan / I'm punching above my weight?

Connie – before you make out I'm a coward. I'm happy with my life.

Tristan Ha! Yeah course you are, you look happy, you look fucking delighted!

Connie You've got no idea how I feel.

Tristan TELL ME!

Connie You're like a child.

Tristan I'm fine for a quick fuck but secretly you want the older, duller man who's gonna *provide* and bring some cash to the fucking table?

Connie Oh my God /

Tristan That's basically what you said –

Connie / what are we even talking about?!

Tristan Gap life!

Connie I'm the one that's sat there and watched you do your cheeky twinkly stuff with the doctor and you were a bit of a sleaze with me early on, what am I supposed to think?!

Tristan I don't – You're the one in a relationship, as you keep going on / about.

Connie *You* go on about it!

Tristan – I'm allowed! I can do what I like!

Connie Oh so I'm a slag now?

Tristan No! Put away your paranoia, love.

Connie Don't call me love. It's so tacky.

Beat.

Tristan Connie. Con. Come on. Kiss and make up.

Connie No, I feel sick.

Tristan I make you sick (?)

Connie I didn't say that. I'm not going to kiss you. I don't want to be sick on you.

Tristan I don't care. Be sick in my mouth. I'll eat it up.

Connie I *said* I feel sick!

Tristan Am I a bit coarse for you? Is that it? Are you used to something more refined? Some wine-drinking chino-wearing cunt?

Connie You don't get to talk about him, you understand?

Tristan I wasn't! Is that what he's like! Came to mind pretty fast!

Connie You keep shaking up my view of him and I think it's manipulative –

Tristan Of course it's fucking manipulative!

Connie You've never met him!

Tristan That's why it's easy to slag him off! Come on, it's a joke!

Connie It's a joke. Your way of getting out of everything. It's a joke. So now I'm a slag with no sense of humour.

Tristan Oh my God, you're insane.

Connie Everything I'm saying makes sense, if there's a problem it's with you understanding!

She makes a gesture of his stupidity. He frustratedly roars at her.

What do you *want* to happen? I mean, really?

Tristan I'll tell you what I want. I don't want to *reason* with you. I want to know right now, in this moment, what you *feel.*

Beat.

Connie I . . . I feel. Oh God. I think I don't love you the way that you love me.

Ow.

Pause.

Tristan Right. Well, you want me to look into the future. Fine. Go home. Suck on his old cock. Stay with him for two years longer than you should, out of guilt for him having left his wife and kid for you –

Connie He didn't –

Tristan Tell yourself you've invested so much now and it was nothing with me and you're getting rougher looking while he's staying the same and he's a good dad and before you know it you're forty-five, fucked and caring for some old cunt with cancer.

Connie *bends double with the pain of it.*

Connie I hate you.

Tristan Have you been calling / him?

Connie / I physically hate you.

Tristan – telling him everything's fine, you miss him. Have you used my fucking phone to do that?!

Connie You gave it to me.

Tristan Give it to me.

Connie I don't have it.

Tristan You're a liar.

Connie You're scaring me.

During, there's a tussle. He gets the phone and practisedly looks through it. He throws it on the floor and smashes it.

Beat.

Connie (*cold*) You just broke your own phone, you stupid Irish cunt.

They physically fight. She ends up getting hurt and this becomes clear.

Stop. Tris.

He sees she is bleeding. She sees she is bleeding. To him it is a tragedy, to her it is a triumph. He backs away, in distress. Then to her, in sorrow.

Tristan I'm sorry. Sorry. It's the drugs.

Connie *Now* it is?!

Tristan (*crying*) I can't handle it.

Connie Stop it.

Tristan I'm losing it.

Connie Bullshit. You're not even on the / drug, Tristan.

Tristan / I'm having a whitey.

He seems about to be sick.

Connie You're not on it. She told me.

Tristan What?

Connie You're on a placebo. This is all just you.

His body tries to absorb the information.

The Pitchfork Disney

Philip Ridley

Philip Ridley was born and grew up in the East End of London. He studied painting at St Martin's School of Art. He has written many highly regarded and hugely influential stage plays: the seminal *The Pitchfork Disney* (published as a Methuen Drama Modern Classic), *The Fastest Clock in the Universe* (winner of a Time Out Award, the Critics' Circle Award for Most Promising Playwright and the Meyer-Whitworth Prize), *Ghost from a Perfect Place* (nominated for the Evening Standard Best New Play Award), *Vincent River* (nominated for the London Festival Fringe Best Play Award), the highly controversial *Mercury Fur*, *Leaves of Glass*, *Piranha Heights* (nominated for the WhatsOnStage Mobius Award for Best Off West End Production), *Tender Napalm* (nominated for the London Fringe Best Play Award), *Shivered* (nominated for the Off-West End Best New Play Award), *Dark Vanilla Jungle* (winner of an Edinburgh Festival Fringe First Award), *Radiant Vermin*, *Tonight with Donny Stixx* and *Karagula* (nominated for the Off-West End Best New Play Award), plus several plays for young people (collectively known as *The Storyteller Sequence*)*: Karamazoo*, *Fairytaleheart*, *Moonfleece* (named as one of the 50 Best Works about Cultural Diversity by the National Centre for Children's Books), *Sparkleshark* and *Brokenville*, as well as *Feathers in the Snow* and *Daffodil Scissors*. He has also directed three feature films from his own screenplays: *The Reflecting Skin* (winner of eleven international awards), *The Passion of Darkly Noon* (winner of the Best Director Prize at the Porto Film Festival) and *Heartless* (winner of the Silver Méliès Award for Best Fantasy Film). In 2012 *What's On Stage* named him a Jubilee Playwright (one of the most influential British writers to have emerged in the past six decades). In 2020, as the COVID-19 pandemic took hold, Philip immediately explored new ways to keep telling stories, writing a sequence of monologues, collectively known as *The Beast Will Rise*, that were all premiered online, one a week, for fifteen weeks. Several of them were subsequently performed at one of the first open-air, socially distanced theatre festivals. Philip has won both the Evening Standard's Most Promising Newcomer to British Film and Most Promising Playwright Awards – the only person ever to receive both prizes.

I DREAMT

I WAS

A DRUM KIT

IN

A

DERELICT

DOWNTOWN

DRIVE

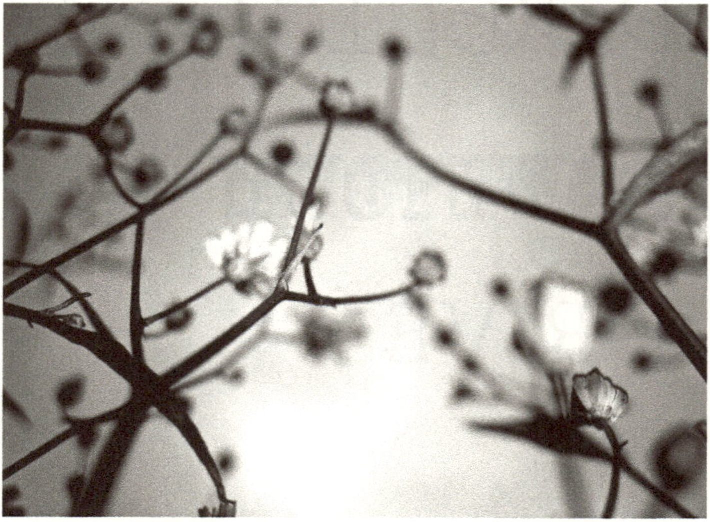

[redacted] eyesore [redacted]

[redacted] jackals [redacted] night?

[redacted] pluck [redacted]

[redacted]

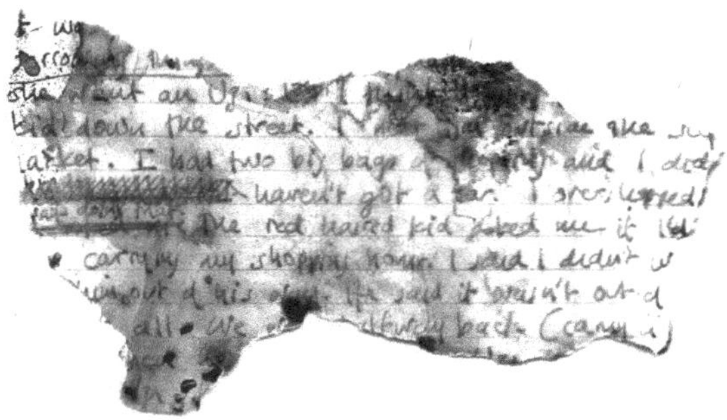

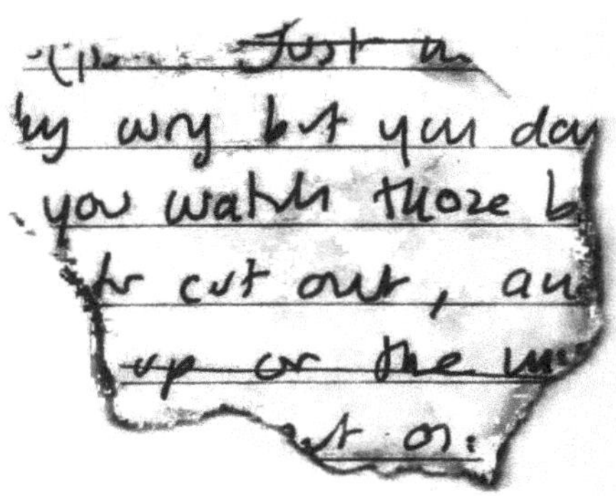

[redacted] rainbows [redacted] eyesore [redacted]
Do jackals [redacted] at night?
If I [redacted] pluck [redacted] sky?
[redacted] trees [redacted] all [redacted]

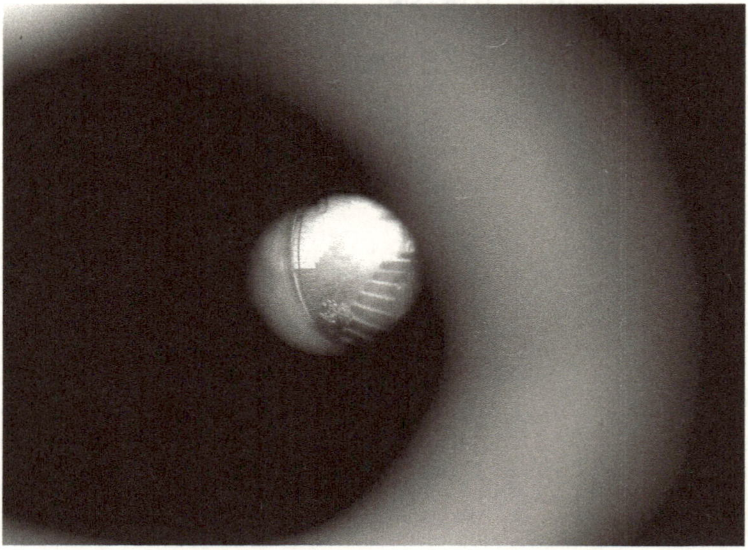

Are rainbows [redacted] eyesore or [redacted]
Do jackals make [redacted] at night?
If I flew [redacted] pluck [redacted] the sky?
The trees I've [redacted] all been [redacted]

[illegible] I'd
[illegible] together. [illegible]
married [illegible] months. We
want to start a fa[illegible] [illegible]
[illegible]. The future loo[illegible]!
Why would he put [illegible]
[illegible]. He wouldn't. No denying
the quiet night world ... ~~He should~~
~~the back~~ I'll [illegible] him two [illegible]
much when I'm going to talk to him

Are rainbows [redacted] eyesore or delight?
Do jackals make [redacted] at night?
If I flew would you pluck [redacted] from the sky?
The trees I've [redacted] have all been bonsai.

We went out with — last night. She's my best
friend. We went to school together. She's an artist.
It was at one of her shows that I met Reg. —
~~was~~ He ~~did the f[illegible] or such~~ made the frames
for her drawings. [illegible]ere beautiful. The frames and
~~[illegible]~~ what was in th[illegible]! — was so happy when
— and Pat [illegible] dating. then ~~going steady~~ ecstatic
[illegible] then — !

me [illegible] [illegible],
when we [illegible] going steady, [illegible] [illegible] night
practically hysterical when we told her we planned
to get married. We ~~were at~~ ~~[illegible]~~ were at the
— that new club down by the canal — and
we danced and had a few drinks — not many,
because Pat + me were seeing Mum today — and
the whole evening was just ... perfect. But when
[illegible] got home, he was a bit ... oh, I
[illegible] ~~[illegible]~~ [illegible] as Yo[illegible]

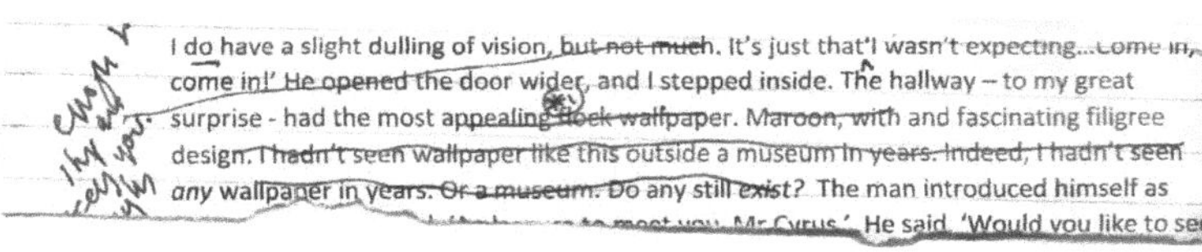

I do have a slight dulling of vision, but not much. It's just that I wasn't expecting...Come in, come in!' He opened the door wider, and I stepped inside. The hallway – to my great surprise - had the most appealing flock wallpaper. Maroon, with and fascinating filigree design. I hadn't seen wallpaper like this outside a museum in years. Indeed, I hadn't seen *any* wallpaper in years. Or a museum. Do any still *exist*? The man introduced himself as

Mr Cyrus.' He said. 'Would you like to see

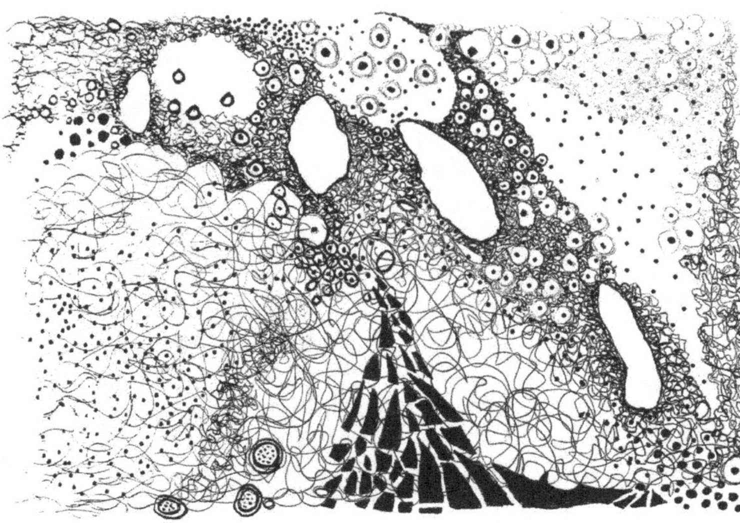

Are rainbows an eyesore or delight?
Do jackals make marmalade at night?
If I flew would you pluck me from the sky?
The trees I've climbed have all been bonsai.

awake

***The Pitchfork Disney* premiered at the Bush Theatre, London, on 2 January 1991.**

The Pitchfork Disney heralded the arrival of a unique and disturbing voice in the world of contemporary drama. Manifesting Philip Ridley's vivid and visionary imagination, and the dark, visceral beauty of his language, the play resonates with his trademark themes: East London, storytelling, moments of shocking violence, distorted memory, fantastical monologues, science fiction and horror references, and that uncanny mix of the barbaric and the beautiful that Ridley had made all his own.

The play was an immediate cause célèbre – enticing a new, younger audience to the theatre – and went on to inspire a whole new movement in theatre (known as `in-yer-face'), ultimately changing the course of British drama.

The Pitchfork Disney now regarded as a seminal masterpiece.

Night. A dimly lit room in the East End of London: front door with many bolts, chest of drawers, table, hard-backed chairs, armchair, doorway leading to kitchen, window. Everything worn and faded.

Presley Stray, *twenty-eight years old, is standing by the window. He is dressed in grungy T-shirt and jeans. He is staring into the darkness outside.*

Haley Stray, *his twin sister, is sitting at the table. She is wearing grungy T-shirt and jeans. She is fiddling with some chocolate wrapping paper.*

Sound of barking dogs from street.

Haley *looks at* **Presley** *anxiously.*

Presley *looks at* **Haley**.

Sound of dogs fades.

Haley Describe it.

Presley Again?

Haley Once more.

Presley You said that last time.

Haley Did I? Don't remember.

Presley Jesus! You said *that* last time too, you know. *And* the time before that. 'Don't remember.' 'Don't remember.'

Haley Why you being so nasty?

Presley Because you blurt out anything to get your own way.

Haley I don't!

Presley You do! Honestly, Haley, sometimes I think you're nothing but a . . . oh, forget it.

Haley No. Say it.

Presley A cheat.

Haley Don't call me that. It's not fair. Not after what *you* did this morning.

Presley What did *I* do?

Haley About the shopping, I mean.

Presley What about it?

Haley The chocolate, Presley. You bought fruit and nut.

Presley So?

Haley You know I don't like fruit and nut. You know it makes me sick. The nuts – they get caught between my teeth. The raisins . . . they . . .

Presley What?

Haley Taste like bits of skin.

Presley How d'you know what skin tastes like?

Haley I can use my imagination.

Presley Well, you *used* to like fruit and nut.

Haley I've *never* liked fruit and nut. *You* like fruit and nut. *My* favourite has always been orange chocolate. You're supposed to buy chocolate for *both* of us. But you don't. You cheat and –

Presley *I* cheat.

Haley Yes! You cheat and only buy fruit and nut for yourself.

Presley But . . . but I didn't *only* buy fruit and nut. I bought other things as well.

Haley What things?

Presley Lots.

Haley You didn't tell me.

Presley I did.

Haley Well, I must've forgotten. Where are they?

Presley Where they always are.

Haley *goes to drawer in sideboard.*

She discovers many bars of different chocolate.

Oh, Presley. You really did. Is that orange chocolate I see? . . . It *is*!

Takes chocolate to table.

Come and have some.

Presley No, thank you.

Haley You're sulking now.

Presley You shouldn't accuse me of cheating.

Haley I'm sorry. It's just that . . . well, I saw you eating a bar of fruit and nut earlier and I assumed – I *wrongly* assumed – that's all there was. I can see now. There's a big selection . . . Come on.

Waves bar temptingly in the air.

Fruit and nut . . . Fruit and nut . . .

Presley *rushes to table.*

They begin to eat.

Presley There's more chocolate than ever in the shops now, Haley. You go in – it sparkles like treasure. Flaky chocolate, mint chocolate, crispy chocolate –

Haley Bubbly chocolate –

Presley Wafer chocolate –

Haley Chocolate with cream in –

Presley Chocolate with nuts in –

Haley Which I don't like!

Presley Which you don't like. All sorts of chocolate in all sorts of paper.

Haley *has been sorting through the pile for another bar of orange chocolate –*

Haley Well, that's typical!

Presley What?

Haley You bought . . . one, two, three, four, five, plus the one you're eating, plus the one this morning, that's *seven* bars of fruit and nut and only *one* bar of orange.

Presley . . . I must have got carried away.

Haley This is just like you, Presley. Sometimes you're so . . . oh, forget it.

Presley No. Say it.

Haley Selfish.

Presley Don't call me that. It's not fair. Not after what *you* did this morning.

Haley What did *I* do?

Presley About who went to get the shopping in the first place.

Haley I . . . I don't understand what you –

Presley It was *your* turn.

Haley Was not!

Presley Was!

Haley Wasn't!

Presley Was! Was!

Haley How? How was it my turn?

Presley I went yesterday.

Haley You did not.

Presley I did. You *know* I did. I bought the milk. And the bread. They were in a brown paper bag. I put them on the table. You were sitting where you're sitting now. You said, 'Didn't you buy any biscuits?' And I said, 'Yes.' I gave them to you. They were in a blue packet. I made you a cup of tea. You dunked the biscuits. Afterwards I put what was left of the biscuits in the fridge.

Haley Biscuits? In the fridge?

Presley Yes.

Haley In a blue packet?

Presley Yes.

Haley A blue packet with yellow and red stripes?

Presley Yes.

Haley That means they're *orange* chocolate biscuits.

Presley I know.

Haley Well, why didn't you tell me? I've felt like an orange chocolate biscuit all day.

Presley You *saw* me put them there.

Haley I forgot. You know what my head's like lately. If you make me a cup of tea and don't offer me a biscuit, then I just assume –

Presley *Stupidly* assume –

Haley *Naturally* assume all the biscuits have gone. I don't think you're hiding them from me.

Presley I wasn't hiding –

Haley You were! You were going to wait for me to take my tablet and fall asleep, then eat them all yourself.

Presley 'Eat them all – '? But I don't even *like* the bloody biscuits. I got them for you. You're just trying to change the subject.

Haley From what?

Presley From why you said it wasn't your turn to get the shopping when you know – know damn well! – it was. Don't you? Eh?

Haley *doesn't answer.*

Presley There! Your silence screams your guilt.

Haley Don't blame me. You . . . you remember what happened last time I went to the shops.

Presley . . . What?

Haley Oh . . . it was terrible.

Presley What was? Tell me.

Slight pause.

Come on.

Haley I . . . I was so scared. I came back crying and shaking. My . . . my clothes were torn.

Presley Torn?!

Haley Yes! There was blood on my legs.

Presley Blood?!

Haley Yes! You wiped it away with a tissue. I was crying so much I couldn't breathe properly. I was hysterical. You remember that, Presley?

Presley I . . . I might do.

Haley You were so nice. You put your arms round me. And I told you everything that had happened. Remember?

Presley Tell me again. Go on. If it's good enough . . . I'll do all the shopping in future.

Haley *All* the shopping?

Presley Every bit.

Haley Till the end of time?

Presley Till the end of time . . . and beyond.

Slight pause.

Haley When I got to the end of the street . . . a pack of dogs appeared. Seven of them. Big, filthy dogs. With maggots in their fur. Foam on their lips. Eyes like clots of blood.

Presley Good, good.

Haley One dog started to sniff me. Its nose was like an ice cube between my legs. Then it started to growl. Lips pulled back over yellow teeth. It started to chase me. I was running. Running and screaming. The other dogs chased me as well. All of them howling and snarling like wolves. They chased me over the waste ground. I fell. Fell into a pile of tin cans. There was a dead cat. My hand went into its stomach. All mushy like rotten fruit. I was screaming. Screaming so loud my throat tasted like blood. One of the dogs bit at my coat. I pulled it away. The coat ripped. I ran and ran. All I could hear was snarling and growling and the sound of my own heart. I ran out of the waste ground. Through the old car park and into the derelict church. Still the dogs chased me. There I was – standing at the altar – with seven rabid animals coming down the aisles towards me. I picked up some old Bibles and threw them. Did no good. The dogs ripped the Bibles to pieces. I was so afraid. And the dogs – they could smell it. My fear. They were attracted by it. They came closer and closer. I could feel their breath against my skin. Hot and reeking of vomit. I backed away. Stumbled up some steps. I wanted to pray. I knew that if I could pray – or sing a hymn – then the dogs would leave me alone. But I couldn't pray. I couldn't sing. All I could do was scream. Then one of the dogs made a lunge for me. I jumped up. Reached above me. Caught hold of something. It was smooth. Cool. Solid. I started to climb. Like climbing a tree. I was halfway up before I realised I was climbing the marble crucifix and my chest was pressed against the chest of Christ. It felt so comforting and safe. Then a dog bit at my feet. Pulled my shoe off. My toes were bleeding. A drop of blood landed in the open mouth of the dog. It went berserk. It started to climb the crucifix. I scarpered higher. Wrapped my legs round the waist of our Saviour. Clung on to the crown of thorns for all I was worth. Then the base of the crucifix started to crumble. It rocked from side to side. Any minute it might fall and send me into the pack of dogs. Like a Christian to the hungry lions. I am so scared. I kiss the lips of Christ. I say, 'Save me! Don't let the crucifix fall!' But the crucifix falls just the same. Crashes to the floor. The dogs nibble at my bloodied fingers. I'm going to be eaten alive. Eaten by savage dogs. 'Help me! Help me!' And then . . . gunshots! I flinch at every one. Look round. The seven dogs are dead. Blood oozing from holes in their skulls. I feel sick. A priest approaches me. He's holding a rifle. He asks if I'm all right. I tell him I am. He says, 'Did you come for confession?' And I say, 'Yes,' because I think that's what he wants to hear and I owe him something for saving my life. So I go into confession with him and he asks me what I've done wrong. I tell him I can't think of anything. He says, 'Don't be stupid. No one's perfect.' I know he's right. I know there's something I've done. Something that made me a naughty girl once. But I can't think of what it is. I tell him I can't think of anything. He tells me to think harder. I can feel him getting angry and frustrated. He wants to forgive me but I'm not giving him the chance. Finally I say, 'I kissed the lips of Christ and they tasted of chocolate.' He calls me a sinner and says I must repent. I ask him if I can be forgiven and he says, 'No! Your sins are too big.' I'm crying when I leave the church. I'm hysterical. Hysterical.

Slight pause.

Presley You'll never have to go shopping again.

Haley Promise?

Presley Promise.

Haley Perhaps we should put it in writing.

Presley Why?

Haley In case you forget.

Presley I won't.

Haley You might.

Presley Jesus, Haley. This is just like you. Sometimes you're so –

Haley What?

Presley Forget it.

Haley No. Tell me.

Presley Suspicious.

Where Do We Live

Christopher Shinn

Christopher Shinn is the author of *Dying City* (Pulitzer Prize finalist), *Where Do We Live* (Obie in Playwriting), *Now or Later* (Evening Standard Theatre Award for Best Play shortlist) and *Four*.

Most recently, his play *Against* premiered at the Almeida Theatre and his adaptation of Ödön von Horváth's *Judgment Day* premiered at Park Avenue Armory. Of his thirteen original plays, over half had their world premiere in England, with five at the Royal Court. Fellowships include the Guggenheim (2005) and the Radcliffe (2019). His plays are published by Methuen Drama and he teaches playwriting at the New School.

What does the word 'crisis' mean to you in a theatrical sense?

I think of a crisis as being anything one's psyche is not able to fully comprehend yet must respond to urgently.

How do you feel theatre has the ability to represent/respond to global crises?

Theatre can represent anything that exists, internally or externally. Whether it can 'respond' to global crises I don't know – it depends on what one means by 'respond'. I am not sure theatre can make much of a material difference by its representations, but it can make a difference in the inner worlds of viewers and readers.

Why did you pick this specific scene? What is this scene doing at this point of the play?

Where Do We Live takes place before and after 9/11 in New York City. I chose this scene between Stephen and Leo because it represents the attempt to integrate trauma into everyday life, which feels apt with the coronavirus pandemic. The scene comes near the end of the play, where the characters' difficulties and failures in integrating trauma begin to press on their psyches.

How does this scene speak beyond the wider context of the play?

Because our 'normal' lives go on even amidst extraordinary disruption, two people navigating desire and intimacy after a shared trauma maps on to many social and political situations.

As a writer, do you feel a point of crisis is always necessary in a play to create/maintain/sustain drama?

By my definition above, I do think crisis is necessary for drama. But the crisis could be purely internal, and needn't affect the broader social setting of the play. Every human being faces crises of different kinds throughout life, some shared, some isolated.

Does theatre as a form allow for a more effective exploration of crisis in terms of what can be explored, presented and communicated to an audience, in relation to other creative forms?

I think theatre is particularly good at dramatising the interpersonal and social ramifications of crisis. Otherwise I don't think it carries any special effectiveness over other forms, and has some significant limitations.

When constructing a play how do you effectively boil down larger global themes that could otherwise be overwhelming for characters within 'their world' so that they can find room to resonate?

I think about how I perceive 'big' events, how they live in my psyche.

What do you feel is the biggest threat to the creation of new drama and plays given the current global crisis? Do we need theatre now more than ever?

The biggest threat to the theatre is that there will be no money for work that doesn't seem likely to be commercially successful. Do we need theatre more than ever? There is so much that we need, I am not sure where theatre would be on my list. We need to become humbler, better educated, more self-critical and more forgiving. Theatre might be a small part of that work.

***Where Do We Live* premiered at the Royal Court Theatre, London in 2002**

In an apartment in lower Manhattan, Stephen spends most of his time writing, looking out of his window and noticing his neighbours. He knows that the black family across the hall survive off benefits and drugs, but now there seem to be more mysterious comings and goings from their apartment.

Set in a post-September 11 world, this searching play asks to what extent is New York's liberal multicultural society under threat and how much should we care about the state in which our neighbours live.

Scene Thirteen

Stephen*'s bedroom.* **Stephen** *and* **Leo** *enter.*

Leo I'm serious, it makes perfect sense. This was Giuliani's greatest fantasy and his greatest fear. He's always had a fascist impulse, which this fits perfectly. But, remember last summer, he had prostate cancer, and there was all that media coverage about how he might be impotent. Months later the two tallest most phallic buildings in New York City go down. What was happening in his body, happening in his city.

Stephen Huh. That's really interesting.

Leo *takes out cocaine, does a bump.* **Leo** *gives* **Stephen** *cocaine.*

Stephen *sniffs cocaine.*

Leo What's funniest is he's just *like* the Taliban – obsessed with forcing his rules, his ideology, violently upon the people: close down the clubs where gays congregate, shut down the strip clubs where women reveal their bodies, cancel funding for art museums who show art that subverts his religious beliefs: he probably *deeply* identifies with the Taliban.

Stephen Right . . .

Leo – Is this the window?

Stephen That's the window.

Leo *looks out the window. Long pause. The sound of a fighter jet passing.*

Leo The F-14s are flying low tonight.

He turns to **Stephen**.

Leo (*brightly*) So. What are we going to do now that we've moved out of a public space and into a private one?

Stephen (*smiling*) Have sex.

Leo *laughs. He looks around and finds a photograph.*

Leo Is this your boyfriend?

Stephen Ex. Yeah.

Leo What was his name?

Stephen Why do you want to know?

Leo I dunno.

Stephen Tyler. I'm gonna brush my teeth.

Leo Okay.

Stephen *exits, off.* **Leo** *stares at the photograph. Then he puts it down and takes off his shoes.* **Stephen** *enters.*

Stephen Hey.

Leo Hey. Have you heard from him since the eleventh?

Stephen Who?

Leo Tyler.

Stephen No . . .

Leo No?

Stephen Nope.

Leo I don't believe in love.

Stephen You don't?

Leo No, I think it's a vague word that is applied indiscriminately.

Stephen (*laughs*) Oh.

Leo To me, a more interesting question is what people are doing to each other in each other's company under the guise of 'love'.

Stephen What do you mean?

Leo Like – what is love? What *is* it? I mean, you can say, okay – okay, this person fucks me, he calls me, he eats meals with me, he tells me about his day, I am in his thoughts and fantasies, I do things and he has feelings about them – you can make a list of facts. But what makes those facts love?

What? And – I couldn't figure it out. So I decided there was no such thing. And that I was fine with that.

Stephen Uh-huh.

Leo *begins removing his clothes.*

Leo The idea of love is so heteronormative, and it's perfect for capitalism: it prevents people from thinking about real problems in their lives, it makes them think, when they feel bad, that something is wrong with them and not the world, it makes people form families and buy things for those families . . . (*He's in his boxers.*) You're so adorable.

Stephen You too.

He turns out the light. We can barely see them. They undress.

Leo Put on some music.

He gets in bed. **Stephen** *puts music on – R&B. He goes into bed.* **Leo** *begins to fellate* **Stephen**, *then kisses him.* **Leo** *gets on top of* **Stephen** *and begins moving.*

Leo Mmm.

Stephen That feels good.

Leo You like that?

Stephen Yeah.

Leo *continues.* **Stephen** *turns him over and gets on top of him and kisses him.*

Leo You can kiss.

Stephen (*laughs*) I can?

Leo Mm-hmm.

They kiss. **Leo** *wraps his legs around* **Stephen**. *Then* **Leo** *takes his own hands and puts them behind his head. He takes* **Stephen**'*s right hand and clasps it to his two hands, as if to restrain them.*

Leo Harder.

Stephen *thrusts against* **Leo** *harder. Then* **Leo** *eases* **Stephen** *off him.* **Leo** *gets on his hands and knees.*

Leo (*sweetly*) Rub against me like you're fucking me.

Stephen *does.*

Leo That's good. Mm.

He masturbates himself as **Stephen** *rubs against him from behind.*

Leo Mmmm.

Stephen Uh. Uh. Uhmm.

He moves more roughly. **Leo** *takes* **Stephen**'*s hand from his breast, puts it on top of his head.*

Leo Pull on my hair a little.

Stephen *does. He arches his neck, kisses* **Leo**.

Leo Mmmm.

Stephen Uhhhh. Uhhhhh.

Leo Mm. You're fine, right?

Stephen What?

Leo I'm fine – we're both fine – you don't have – you don't have / HIV.

Stephen No.

Leo *More.* Oh God.

Stephen *continues, getting rougher.*

Stephen You like that?

Leo *Yes.*

Stephen Yeah? You like that?

Leo – Fuck me.

Stephen Yeah, you want me to fuck you?

Leo Yes please.

Stephen Yeah?

Leo I like it.

Stephen I like it too. Uh. Uh.

Leo Go inside me.

Stephen Yeah?

Leo You can go inside me.

Stephen (*stopping for a moment*) Wait – go? – literally?

Leo Please fuck me.

Stephen I / don't –

Leo Please.

Pause. Then **Stephen** *enters him, somewhat awkwardly.* **Leo** *grimaces a little.* **Stephen** *fucks him, slow at first, then faster.*

Leo Oh my *God* . . . Oh *God* . . . Oh *God* . . .

Stephen Uhhhhh. Uhhhh, uhhh uhhh –

Leo Mmmm mm mmm –

Stephen Uhh / uhh uhh –

Leo Mmm mmm mmm mmm / mmm mmm mmm –

Stephen Uhhhm uuhmm uhuuhmm –

He stops suddenly.

Leo What? Did you come?

Pause. **Stephen** *releases, lies back on the bed.*

Stephen No . . .

Leo Why did you stop?

Stephen I'm sorry.

Pause. **Leo** *grabs* **Stephen***'s penis and begins to masturbate him.*

Stephen I'm sorry, I have to stop.

Pause. **Leo** *lies back, masturbates himself. Sound of a fighter jet cutting across the sky. Finally* **Leo** *orgasms.*

Leo Uhhhhh –

Pause.

Stephen Let me get you a towel.

He gets **Leo** *a towel and gives it to him.* **Leo** *cleans himself.* **Stephen** *turns off music and dresses.* **Leo** *puts the towel on the floor and dresses. As they do this:*

Stephen That was interesting, the comparisons you were making before with the Taliban and Giuliani.

Leo Uh-huh?

Stephen I've been reading about Afghanistan – the chaos of the region. So many tribes – so many different groups – disconnected, historically, from their / central government.

Leo Right.

Stephen Disconnected from their leaders – and disconnected from each other – all these various groups occupying the same space without being able to / find a common –

Leo Uh-huh.

Stephen Just – how fractured and isolated they are – like New York, too, in some ways . . .

Pause. **Leo** *and* **Stephen** *are dressed.* **Leo** *looks at* **Stephen**.

Leo Nice to meet you.

Stephen You're gonna go?

Leo *smiles.*

Stephen Are you sure? I could make some tea . . .

Leo I'm fine. Bye.

He goes, off. **Stephen** *sits down on his bed. He looks out the window.*

Motortown

Simon Stephens

Simon Stephens began his theatrical career in the literary department of the Royal Court Theatre, where he ran its Young Writers' Programme.

His plays for theatre include *Bluebird* (Royal Court Theatre, London, 1998, directed by Gordon Anderson); *Herons* (Royal Court Theatre, 2001); *Port* (Royal Exchange Theatre, Manchester, 2002); *One Minute* (Crucible Theatre, Sheffield, 2003 and Bush Theatre, London, 2004); *Christmas* (Bush Theatre, 2004); *Country Music* (Royal Court Theatre Upstairs, 2004); *On the Shore of the Wide World* (Royal Exchange Theatre and National Theatre, London, 2005); *Motortown* (Royal Court Theatre Downstairs, 2006); *Pornography* (Deutsches Schauspielhaus, Hanover, 2007; Edinburgh Festival/Birmingham Rep, 2008 and Tricycle Theatre, London, 2009); *Harper Regan* (National Theatre, 2008); *Sea Wall* (Bush Theatre, 2008/Traverse Theatre, Edinburgh, 2009); *Heaven* (Traverse Theatre, 2009); *Punk Rock* (Lyric Hammersmith, London, and Royal Exchange Theatre, 2009); *The Trial of Ubu* (Essen Schauspielhaus/ Toneelgroep Amsterdam, 2010); *A Thousand Stars Explode in the Sky* (co-written with David Eldridge and Robert Holman; Lyric Hammersmith, London, 2010); *Marine Parade* (co-written with Mark Eitzel; Brighton International Festival, 2010); *T5* (Traverse Theatre, 2010); and *Wastwater* (Royal Court Theatre Downstairs, 2011).

Awards include the Pearson Award for Best New Play, 2001, for *Port*; Olivier Award for Best New Play for *On the Shore of the Wide World*, 2005; and for *Motortown* German critics in *Theater Heute*'s annual poll voted him Best Foreign Playwright, 2007. His adaptation of *The Curious Incident of the Dog in the Night-Time* won the 2015 Tony Award for Best Play.

What does the word 'crisis' mean to you in a theatrical sense?

I think it's quite an exciting word. I'm quite inspired by the theories of Edward Bond and his approach to define and philosophise drama. One of the things that Bond talks about is the 'theatre of accident'. He tells a story of having a crash on the motorway in the late sixties in the early years of motorways in Britain, his car being sent into a tailspin but he was able to control it, thankfully. He talks about the experience of being in a car in the middle of a tailspin. He says the physiological experience was one of extreme clarity – that he could suddenly see everything in his world with more clarity than he had ever seen before, he could see the detail of things and the colours of things. He talks about seeing the colours of the tie on the driver of the car that hit him. He found subsequent to this a great metaphor of what great drama is, in terms of an alertness and an energy that he felt himself experience. For him it became important that drama existed in what he called an 'emergency time' or an 'accident time'. It's in an emergency that our bodies are more alert, it's in emergency or crisis when our synapses are firing and our pores are more open, our brains are awake. So on one hand this particular crisis is a catastrophe and it breaks my heart. Theatres will close, people will die, in this country far more people are dying than need to die because of the ineptitude of government which is particularly heart-breaking. But at the same time there's an oddity to this moment that I find fascinating. Tim Crouch talks about this in a poem that he wrote for YouTube – he talks about the strangeness of this time being very beautiful. So for me, crisis covers not just an instability of the most profound order but also the possibility for seeing the world which we've known and been familiar with, with a clarity and alertness that we haven't seen before. There's something kind of beautiful about that I think.

How do you feel theatre has the ability to represent/respond to global crises?

I guess for me theatre is the most human of the art forms. It's the most human in its creation and the most human in its reception. It's that humanness that it offers that means that it makes sense of the world, whether that world is in crisis or trauma or not, or with a particular directness that other art forms don't have. It's being present with other people and being in the same room in a way that can't be replicated or experienced in any other time. This is clearly one of the key structural problems of theatre during this time as key to it is the assembly of strangers. That's the thing we're not going to be able to have for some time. That will be a hard thing to return to. We don't read a novel with 300 people in the same moment. We don't watch television with 300 people simultaneously or watch a movie that can never be replicated. Music and visual art don't engage with story in the same way. The way in which it uses story and the assembly of strangers to consume it makes it the most particular of art forms. I think it will survive this, I do think that, but I think it took a long time to establish post-Second World War theatre from the formation of the Arts Council to the formation of the Royal Court Theatre – that took ten years. It could be an interruption, given that we have experienced what theatre is maybe we'll find a new version of what theatre can be.

Why did you pick this specific scene? What is this scene doing at this point of the play?

In this scene Danny, the protagonist of the play, takes a BB gun that he bought from a friend of his in Southend and he takes it to a guy called Paul in Canning Town who lives with a teenage girl called Jade. Paul doctors the gun to make it fire live ammunition. It's a scene that frightened me to write. I went to places of crisis and catastrophe that I've not been to before as a writer, I dared myself to write things that I'd not written before in the writing of this scene. It seems to have been a scene that came out not just from the emotional catastrophe of the second Iraq War but a particular emotional experience of someone serving in that war, or the psycho-geography of a country who sent young people to serve and die in that war, but also the decade of a war on terror. That scene somehow captures the unpredictability and the volatility and fear of that decade I think. I remember really vividly seeing it rehearsed for the first time and asking myself what the fuck have I written, because the scene seemed so alarming. More recently there was a very good production directed by Michael Fentiman at the Royal Welsh College of Music and Drama. It's the scene that's the hardest for the students to engage in. They were frightened by it, they were appalled by it; appalled by its racial politics, by its gender politics and frightened by the play. I thought there was something profound in that, it is a frightening scene. I sometimes think that the function of drama is to frighten. Another thing that Edward Bond said to me is that it's the job of the dramatist to create psychosis on stage so that the audience need less experience of it in their life. In a way it was reassuring to me that fifteen years later that this play and this scene still seemed to resonate and frighten and unsettle and unnerve people in a moment defined by other catastrophes and other crises.

How does this scene speak beyond the wider context of the play?

You've got a few things at play. Converting the gun to fire live ammunition brings mortality to the stage. When drama makes you consider how people die I think that it resonates beyond the specificity of the world of the play. The injustice and questionable morality through Paul's relationship with Jade and then Danny's fascination with Jade are the things that really unsettle people. I think Paul's spirit of fascination and enquiry, his didacticism, his consistent fascination with the horrors of the world he is living in, coupled with his own broken and bad morality, means that his particular investigation of the transgression which he brings to the stage and what he might take part in, I think that really frightens people.

Does theatre as a form allow for a more effective exploration of crisis in terms of what can be explored, presented and communicated to an audience, in relation to other creative forms?

The humanness, the liveness, the volatility, the awareness that something is happening in the room and something is going on and that it's a time-based medium. Unlike any other form of literature it's so dependent on the element of time, perhaps performance poetry. When you're reading a novel the reader is in charge of how long it lasts. The reader has agency. For a play and a play in performance in the theatre it's the artists who have that agency and it's that that gives it its notion of mortality. I think that's what gives it its uniqueness.

When constructing a play how do you effectively boil down larger global themes that could otherwise be overwhelming for characters within 'their world' so that they can find room to resonate?

I would say two things about that. For me plays always come from a position of fear or uncertainty. They come from questions I don't know the answers to. As long as those questions and those fears and the uncertainty that I'm forcing myself to look at, as long as they play out in a broad enough context, I think those themes and those worlds and those questions will percolate into the world of the play. As long as I'm thinking broadly enough they'll be in there somewhere. My plays tend to be set in a fictional version of a real world, a recognisable fictionalised version of the real world. *Motortown* was set in a fictional version of Dagenham. It's Dagenham and it's Essex and it's Southend. They are real places and that allows me as a writer to explore real questions and real things. The really technical answer to that is as long as what the characters are saying has an action as well as content, as long as it's not just what they are saying but it's also what they are *doing* to each other, as long as you've done the job to make sure that every line has a charge, has an action, then you can bring all kinds of themic investigation into it and I think that's what Paul does, that's what I tried to do with him at all times. Have a character that's asking appalling questions, unthinkable and unbearable theories, but as long as he was always doing something to Danny then he can instigate and investigate those themes. As long as the action is there then they can inform the ideas.

What do you feel is the biggest threat to the creation of new drama and plays given the current global crisis?

Just the theatres staying open. I don't really think that I'm anxious that people will lose their appetite for new plays or that people will not want to go to the theatre or that people will want plays of a particular type. I don't think those things are true. I think people will be as hungry for plays which are pushing and difficult and volatile as they have been. There may be a few months where people are self-conscious about it. If anything it makes you aware how extraordinary the experience of watching theatre is. I think the only thing that's going to stop it is if the government doesn't step up. I think any other government would, but not this government.

***Motortown* premiered at the Royal Court Theatre, London in April 2006**

Danny returns from Basra to a foreign England and a different kind of battle. He visits an old flame, buys a gun and goes on a blistering road trip through the new home front.

'I don't blame the war. The war was alright. I miss it. It's just you come back to this.'

Written during the London bombings of 2005, *Motortown* is a fierce, violent and controversial response to the anti-war movement – and to the war itself. Chaotic and complex, powerful and provocative, it portrays a volatile and morally insecure world.

Scene Four

Danny, **Paul** *and* **Jade**.

Paul To ask about the meaning of life is about as philosophically interesting as asking about the meaning of wood or the meaning of grass. There is no meaning. Life is, as science has proven in the last two years, a genetic system. An arrangement of molecular structure. There is no solidity.

Only a perception of solidity. There is no substance. Only the perception of substance. There is no space. Only the perception of space. This is a freeing thing, in many ways, Danny. It means I can be anywhere. At anytime. I can do anything. I just need to really try. This is Jade. Say hello, Jade.

Jade Hello.

Danny Hello.

Paul How's Tom doing?

Danny He's all right, I think.

Paul Good man. Good man. Good man. He's a bit of a weird old cunt though, don't you think?

Danny I do, sometimes.

Paul He is. He speaks very highly of you, but he is a bit of a weird old cunt.

Danny (*to* **Jade**, *lying*) Jade was my wife's name.

Paul Are you married, Danny?

Danny I was.

Paul How old are you?

Danny Twenty-seven.

Paul What happened to your wife, Danny?

Danny She got killed.

Paul No.

Danny We got robbed. She got shot in the chest.

Paul Good God, Danny, that's awful.

Danny Yeah.

Paul When was this?

Danny A couple of years ago.

Paul Did they catch the fucker?

Danny Yeah. He was a soldier. Some squaddie.

Paul For God's sake. I'm really sorry to hear that. Aren't you, Jade? Aren't you sorry to hear that?

Jade Yeah. I am.

Paul We're both of us really sorry to hear that, Danny.

A long pause.

Yes.

Is it Danny or Daniel?

Danny Danny.

Paul Good. How boyish! What do you do, Danny?

Danny What do I do?

Paul Your job, what is it?

Danny I'm in film. I do special effects for films.

Paul Do you really? That's rather remarkable to me! What a remarkable job. What films have you done?

Danny None that you know.

Paul Go on. Try me. I go to the cinema all the time, don't I, Jade?

Jade Yeah. He does.

Danny I worked on a few of the Bond movies. I worked on the gun scenes on some of the Bond films.

Paul Which ones?

Danny *Die Another Day*. Mainly.

Paul I never saw that. Did I?

Jade No.

Paul I hate James Bond. I think his films are fucking dreadful. Did you come in on the train?

Danny I did, yeah.

Paul I like the train ride. Out of Dagenham.

Danny Yeah.

Paul I like Dagenham.

Danny Do yer?

Paul It's full of fat kids in football shirts, isn't it? Lovely that. I like it round here more, though. I like the views, you understand?

Danny I do.

Paul Canning Town. London, E16. Do you like London, Danny?

Danny I'm not sure.

Paul You're not sure?!

Danny It's a bit big for me.

Paul A bit big. (*He smiles.*) You see, that's the problem with the Essex native, though, Danny, isn't it? They never fucking leave.

Danny That's not completely true.

Paul What's the furthest you've ever been to?

Danny You what?

Paul In the world?

Danny France.

Paul Is it?

Danny Yeah.

Paul Ha!

Jade *smirks too.*

Danny Don't laugh.

Paul No. You're right. I'm being rude. I'm sorry. It's just I'm quite the traveller. I travel almost constantly. I'm more familiar with aeroplanes than I am with buses. That's actually the truth. Do you want to know something about aeroplanes?

Danny Go on.

Paul You know the real reason why people tell you to adopt the brace position in the event of an emergency on an aeroplane? It's so the impact of the crash on the neck forces the spinal column into the skull and into the brain and kills you immediately. Rather than allowing you to suffer a prolonged and horrible death. That's the reason why, really.

Danny This is my gun.

He pulls his gun out of his pocket and shows it to him.

Paul Yes. Put it away. We'll sort that out in a bit. Can I get you a cup of tea, Danny?

Danny No thank you.

Paul Or a coffee? Or a beer? A whisky? Anything like that?

Danny A water.

Paul A water? You want a glass of water? Tap or mineral?

Danny Tap.

Paul Tap water. Very good. Ice? Lemon?

Danny No thank you.

Paul As it comes, as it were. Terrific. Jade, sweetheart, get Danny a glass of water, will you? There's a good girl.

Jade *leaves. They watch her go.*

Paul She's fourteen. You wouldn't think it to look at her, would yer?

Danny I don't know.

Paul You wouldn't. Immoral really, but . . .

A long pause. **Paul** *stares at* **Danny**.

Paul Can I ask you this? Do you ever get that feeling? When you're in, you're in, you're in, say a, a, a, a bar or a restaurant or walking down a street, and you see a girl. A teenage girl.

You see the nape of her neck. In her school uniform. With her friends. All pigtailed. And you just want to reach out and touch. You ever get that?

Danny I'm not sure.

Paul You see, when you can't tell the difference any more between what is real and what is a fantasy. That's frightening, I think.

They don't let you take anything onto planes anymore, Danny. Did you know that? Since 9/11. Fucking nothing. Apart from pens, oddly. They should take pens off you. That's what I think. The pen can be a lethal instrument. You can stab somebody in the eye. Push it all the way in. Cripple them at least. Cut into the brain. Leave them brain-damaged. It'd be easy, that. I'd leave the end sticking out, wouldn't you?

Danny I don't know.

Paul You would. I would. It would look hilarious. I need a shave.

You know what I think about 9/11, Danny?

Danny No, I'm actually in a bit of a –

Paul Wait for your fucking drink!

Danny –

Paul *glares at him.*

Paul The best heist film Hollywood never made. That's what I think. The level of planning, the level of daring, the downright fucking scientific sexiness and brass-balled braveness that went into that operation! Christ! You should tell your friends. They could cast it up! Cast Bruce Willis. Black him up a bit. That'd be a fucking blockbuster all right.

Danny Yeah.

Paul They should make films out of everything, I think. Films and musicals. They should make musicals out of everything as well. Imagine it! *Bulger! The Musical!* I'd pay forty quid to see that.

Jade *returns. She gives* **Danny** *a glass of water.*

Danny Thank you very much.

Jade That's all right.

Paul *waits for* **Danny** *to drink. Watches him.*

Paul How is it? Your water?

Danny It's fine, thanks.

Paul Look out there. Have you the slightest idea how many tube lines run under the square mile area you can see from out of that window, Danny, have you? It's completely fucking hollow down there. Beneath the surface of the ground. It's full of vermin and metal. Rats. Mice. Squirrels.

Foxes. Soon there'll be dogs fucking everywhere. Stray dogs. Little pit bulls. Wandering around. They'll come in down the river. And then, in the future, in London, people will find foxes in their living rooms. You'll have to batter them with your broom sticks.

Or shoot them in the head. Either method works just as well. Scabby fucking things. They'll eat your cat as soon as look at you. I'm gonna bring hunting for foxes with hounds back.

But not in fucking Surrey. Not in Wiltshire. Down Oxford Street. A huge fucking pack of us.

He makes the noise of a hunting trumpet.

Show me.

Danny *shows him his gun.*

Paul P99. Nice. Let me have a look.

He opens a small toolkit, takes out a tiny screwdriver and a tape measure and opens the gun. Goes to work adjusting it. He wears half-moon spectacles as he does so.

The notion of a War on Terror is completely ingenious. It is now possible to declare war on an abstraction. On an emotional state.

He continues to work.

God. Law. Money. The left. The right. The church. The state. All of them lie in tatters. Wouldn't you be frightened?

He continues to work.

The only thing we can do is feast ourselves on comfort foods and gobble up television images. Sport has never been more important. The family unit seems like an act of belligerence. *All* long-term relationships are doomed or ironic. Therefore sexuality must be detached. But, because of fucking AIDS, detached sexuality is suicidal. So everybody goes online.

Hardcore black fucking MPEG porn . . . junky lesbian breast torture . . . bondage fantasies, hardcore pics . . . free bestiality stories, low-fat diet, free horse-sex, torture victims zoo . . .

Marvellous stuff!

You can get all the free trailers. And that's enough for me.

I wouldn't spend any fucking money on it. That's just a waste, I think. I think that's when you're addicted to it.

He continues to work.

I saw a fifty-year-old man sit a sixteen-year-old Brummie girl on his lap. He held her breast in his hand and got her to smile at the webcam. Asked her what she thought all of the people watching did while she masturbated. She said she thought they masturbated. It was a truthful image. It sits in my consciousness.

He looks up at **Danny** *and points with his tiny screwdriver.*

Paul You want to know the truth about the poor in this country? They're not cool. They're not soulful. They're not honest. They're not the salt of the fucking earth. They're thick. They're myopic. They're violent. They're drunk most of the time. They like shit music. They wear shit clothes. They tell shit jokes. They're racist, most of them, and homophobic the lot of them. They have tiny parameters of possibility and a minuscule spirit of enquiry or investigation. They would be better off staying in their little holes and fucking each other.

And killing each other.

They're on the way there already, of course. There's a guy who lives downstairs. He got himself involved in all that. Couple of fellahs come along. Cut his biceps in half with a pair of garden shears. Absolutely extraordinary.

Every week entire towns are torn apart by the puking boozers and the French-cropped cunts of England. Whacked off their heads on customised National Health prescription anti-depressants. And testosterone injections. And Turkey Twizzlers. They puke up in the lobbies of banks. They use their bank cards to go and puke in a bit of peace and quiet. Leave it there. Welcome to Barclays!

And the girls are so vapid. You know the type? All brown skin and puppy fat and distressed denim on their arses and ponchos.

He continues to work.

When Jade's gone I think I'm going to start spending my time in the bars of Borough Market. Or Sloane Street. Or Bloomsbury. Get myself a rich girl, a business girl. You see them. And below their suits and their handbags and their fresh, fresh skin and clean hair, you know, you just fucking know.

Royalty are the worst, of course. Mind you, if I was the king of this country I'd start every morning with a blowjob too. From my butler. With my coffee and my yoghurt and my fruit. It's the most civilised thing I can imagine. It's absolutely legendary.

Wait here.

He leaves. **Danny** *drinks his water.* **Jade** *shifts her position. He looks at her.*

Danny Will he be long?

Jade I don't know.

Pause.

Danny Doesn't he do your head in after a while?

Jade What do you mean?

Danny He goes on a bit, doesn't he?

Jade I like him.

Danny Is he your boyfriend?

Jade Ha!

Danny What's funny?

Jade 'Is he your boyfriend?'

Danny What's funny about that?

Jade Nothing. It doesn't matter.

Danny You shouldn't laugh at people. Shouldn't laugh at me, definitely. Shouldn't you be at school?

Jade I don't go to school anymore.

Danny Why not?

Jade It's boring. I don't need to, anyway. Paul teaches me all kinds of stuff.

Danny I can imagine.

I used to go Eastbrook. In Dagenham. You ever heard of it?

Jade No.

Danny It's a fucking remarkable place. For a thousand reasons. But I never really felt completely comfortable there, you with me?

Jade –

Danny I always wanted to go out. See, you'd get a day like this. Go down the docks. Fuck that lot. Go and watch the river. Go over the Chase. Don't you think, Jade?

Jade –

Danny Have a day trip. We should have a day trip. Us two. Me and you, Jade. What do you think?

Jade I don't think Paul would like it.

Danny He wouldn't mind. Would he?

Paul *comes back in with the gun complete.*

Danny Would you, Paul? Would you mind if I took Jade for a day trip? Hop in the car. Go to the seaside.

Paul *looks at him for a long time. Hands him back his gun.*

Paul Do you need ammunition?

Danny I do, yeah.

Paul Here. 125 gram, nine-millimetre standard pressure hollow-point. Fifty rounds, ten pounds. Sixty pounds total. That's a very good price.

Danny Thank you.

Paul *hands him a small, plain, red box.* **Danny** *hands him sixty pounds. He examines his gun with a confidence and proficiency that belies the notion that he is anything other than a soldier.*

Paul This weather.

Danny Yeah.

Paul This whole planet is in a terrible state, Danny, you know? The ecological fallout of the decisions that you have made – you, Danny, personally, today, you, not anybody else, you – the ecological fallout of those decisions is catastrophic. And it's the same for all of us. Times sixty million. Times six billion. And nobody says anything about it. There are too many people. There is not enough water. There is not enough oxygen. And nobody admits it. And so now we're gonna consume China. And then we're gonna consume India and then we're gonna consume Africa and we'll carry on consuming. We'll continue to eat it all up and eat it all up and eat it all up until the only thing we've got left to fucking eat, Danny, the only thing we've got left to eat is each other.

Manchester from The Mysteries

Chris Thorpe

Chris Thorpe is a writer and performer from Manchester, where he has an ongoing association with the Royal Exchange Theatre – work for them includes *There Has Possibly Been an Incident* and *The Mysteries*. Other theatre work includes *Victory Condition* and *The Milk of Human Kindness* for the Royal Court Theatre, *Chorus* for the Gate Theatre and *Hannah*, *Beowulf* and one of *Aesop's Fables* for the Unicorn Theatre. He also has ongoing collaborations with Rachel Chavkin produced by China Plate (*Confirmation*/*Status*), Lucy Ellinson (TORYCORE), Portugal's malavoadora (*Overdrama*/*House-Garden*/*Dead End*/*Your Best Guess*) and Hannah Jane Walker (*The Oh Fuck Moment*/*I Wish I Was Lonely*). Chris was a founder member of Unlimited Theatre, is an Associate of Live Art/Theatre company Third Angel and has worked frequently with Forest Fringe. He also collaborates with Rachel Bagshaw, writing the award-winning *The Shape of the Pain*, recently adapted for BBC as *Where I Go (When I Can't Be Where I Am)*. He has also worked as a translator, most frequently with Serbian playwright Ugljesa Sajtinac and Belarus Free Theatre. His short film for the Royal Court and the Financial Times about the climate crisis, *What Do You Want Me to Say?*, was released in September 2019.

Current work includes the Methuen Climate Commission for the Royal Court, *Dying* for mala voadora and the National Theatre of Portugal, *Tell Me*, for HOME Manchester, co-written with Yusra Warsama, a new piece for Nationaltheater Mannheim in collaboration with Javaad Alipoor, *Hold Out Your Hand*, a play for young performers produced by Scottish company Wonder Fools and the Traverse Theatre, and *A Family Business*, his next collaboration with Rachel Chavkin. He also works closely with the National Student Drama Festival.

What does the word `crisis' mean to you in a theatrical sense?

I suppose there's a classic scene-based example of what a crisis is for a character, or what a crisis is in terms of the arc of a narrative and its position within that, but I don't really think of it in those terms. I think it's a point in time you have the liberty to craft in a live experience, which brings everyone in the room into a new relationship with their own decision making. Now that can be situational, it can be about a situation you have described which everyone is then informed on and everyone to a greater or lesser degree gets to be there, even participate, whilst that situation resolves itself. Or it could be something much more internally active, whereby what you've created with the words you've written, or the environment in which the words are in, or the situation which you've put everyone in, is a genuinely felt moment of uncertainly about what is going to happen next. There's an individual awareness of the collective power of decision making that we are employing at these points to explore how a situation might change and what we're going to do about it. That's how I understand crisis, in terms of a moment where agency becomes apparent, consciously crafted to exist in any piece of art that I'm making.

How do you feel theatre has the ability to represent/respond to global crises?

Weirdly I think that one of things that theatre tries to do, which it's not necessarily that good at, is tell stories about crisis. I'm not convinced that's the best use of the tools of theatre. I also am not sure that theatre can be educational in the sense of giving people the information and facts and figures of a crisis. I think there are better channels for both of those things. But the massive advantage theatre has is the physical presence of active minds that can be put in a position where they can look at themselves. What theatre is really good at is laying out both the feeling of and the structure of (maybe a microcosm of) a crisis in a room, and stretching time and viewpoint to allow people in that to room look at how their minds respond to these conditions in real time. To look at their own psychology. And yes, sometimes, some of the tools we can employ to do that are character or story or information, but actually that content is not the most important thing in terms of theatre's ability to talk about crisis. The thing that should have primacy is our collective presence in that room and the way we can take a step out of the normal rules of being in the world and look at our own minds and the frameworks that surround them.

Why did you pick this specific scene? What is this scene doing at this point of the play?

I think I chose it because it's something where a real-world event or crisis is so clearly present. It's an extract of the sixth of six plays about six different communities. The largest community in that cycle of plays is Manchester, which is where I'm from. It is one of those plays that centres on a specific event – because Manchester is such a big place it was useful to have that shared event (the Manchester Arena bombing) at the heart of it. It helps to focus us on how communities react to crisis. So in terms of the Arena bombing the extract very clearly refuses to describe the detail but describes the moment that the city was plunged into crisis by a single event and the immediate reaction of that city. Then does that thing I was just talking about, takes a step back and says, 'But this isn't just about detailing our immediate reaction or describing the event that we're talking about, it's about taking a pause to say how did we react and what are the failures in our reaction to it.'

There are amazing things that we can detail and we should detail in the reaction to an attack like that, primarily the capacity of humanity to come together as a community, to step in and help the human beings who are immediately affected by it. But when that initial shock then spreads over time and over space throughout the whole of that community, and when the psychology of that need to help becomes sentimentalised and collectivised in terms of our view of ourselves as a city, who is excluded from that? What are the shorthand ways we use to symbolise that solidarity and concern that actually take us out of a useful reaction to that moment of crisis? They can maybe cut off further widespread collective action to address the causes of that crisis, or to acknowledge things about that crisis that we own more than we like to think we do. The young man who bombed the Arena on that night being from Manchester, for example, which he was; irrespective of what his personal heritage or the religion of his family is, he was Mancunian. What is it about the way that we react to a crisis, in this city that tells a very strong story about itself, that actually won't let us go to the places where we're able to talk about that fact that he was one of ours? What the extract does is detail the event and then start to look at the frameworks around the reaction, to look at how the reaction to that crisis twists itself into shapes that maybe aren't ultimately as useful as they could be. This is something I think theatre does really well. It allows us to be there while we slow down, look at and unpick our collective reaction to moments of crisis, and question them.

As a writer, do you feel a point of crisis is always necessary in a play to create/maintain/sustain drama?

I'd argue that even ideas of narrative or character aren't necessary. What I think is necessary a moment of collective awareness of how our minds work, which for me comes as much from form and presence as the need for `drama'. If you want to characterise that moment as a crisis, then that's where I think crisis is necessary in theatre.

Does theatre as a form allow for a more effective exploration of crisis in terms of what can be explored, presented and communicated to an audience, in relation to other creative forms?

I think theatre's given more latitude by more people to slip outside of the forms of narrative. That's a choice which we have when we write theatre, to explore crisis through form, which we still don't exercise as much as we should.

When constructing a play how do you effectively boil down larger global themes that could otherwise be overwhelming for characters within `their world' so that they can find room to resonate?

Detail and honesty. And the form of language as much as subject. It's quite a short answer but I would say one tiny detail or set of details shared in the right form, be that form repetitive or physical or verbal or whatever form you're using, one tiny detail very clearly shared with everyone in the room is a more effective way of bringing those people together than a huge broad-brush overview of a `global' situation. We need to operate, during a show, on the same information or at least think we share the same information and a way to get into that is to really focus in on details. So quite often I separate out and focus on a much smaller detail of a bigger picture, temporally, linguistically, in terms of whose head we're in when we're observing it.

What do you feel is the biggest threat to the creation of new drama and plays given the current global crisis? Do we need theatre now more than ever?

I worry that we'll fall back into traditional modes of storytelling and I think that doing that has the potential to exclude a load of voices who already struggle to be represented in the mainstream, either because of their heritage or their ethnicity or the part of society that they're starting off from. I don't worry about that with the organisations I've been working with recently but I do think across the whole industry there might be a kickback towards the traditional and safe, which is going to make the whole place much less exciting. I think we have a pretty good chance of avoiding that – there's power in writers collectively to not allow that to happen. As with anything, when working in theatre the first thing you have to do is resist internalising a kind of hierarchy. I think one of the reasons that a lot of us do what we do is that we're resistant to working in that way, in a hierarchical situation anyway. Of course what happens is, as soon as we start working we realise we've internalised those ideas of hierarchy so we're unconsciously ranking people against each other because of the forms they choose, because of the subjects they choose, because of the places they work. I think one of the things that's going to avoid that slide back towards more conservative choice-making is a conscious effort on the part of writers to keep alive the opportunity to elevate forms and ways of talking that aren't even necessarily invented yet. It starts with resisting the things that you yourself have internalised and I think if we keep our eyes on doing that, it's going to help to resist going back to, for want of a better word, traditional way of doing things.

The Mysteries premiered at Manchester Royal Exchange in October 2018

Chris Thorpe's cycle of six, warm, witty new plays crosses northern England, from a sheep farm in Eskdale via a tourist information centre in Whitby to Manchester.

A fort on a hilltop, a landowner's estate, a tourist information office, a bird sanctuary, a re-developed factory, a public square, silent and remembering. Chris Thorpe's cycle of six new plays explores the landscapes that surround us and how we live with each other.

The concert starts, it is spectacular
The concert ends, the crowd are happy
The young man wanders thoughtless through the foyer
Stands with his backpack, briefly imagines
A small bird pinned to a vast sky
And –
And I could describe this, but I won't
I could bring language to bear on this
Freeze the moment in words of horror
Name the victims, state their ages
Describe the chemistry, the sound it makes
The effect of the fragments
The sight of the aftermath
I could describe it all in detail, but I won't
Better to concentrate on this
The homeless ran to offer help
The paramedics ran to offer help
The nurses ran to offer help
The surgeons ran to offer help
The parents ran to offer help
The police ran to offer help
The women ran to offer help
The men ran to offer help
The cleaners ran to offer help
The foreigners ran to offer help
The kebab shop workers ran to offer help
The drunks ran to offer help
The developers ran to offer help
The criminals ran to offer help
The shop assistants ran to offer help
The landlords ran to offer help
The sex workers ran to offer help
The religious ran to offer help
The non-believers ran to offer help
The train drivers ran to offer help
The musicians ran to offer help
The designers ran to offer help
The hipsters and the taxi drivers
The boxers and the pilots
The soldiers and the editors
The journalists and students

The secretaries and the t-shirt sellers
The accountants and the ticket touts
The teenagers and grandparents
The city ran towards still present danger
The whole city opened its houses and its flats
People were the best of themselves
This city's people were the best of themselves

And the next day the tens of thousands gather
And they are the best of themselves too
To say love conquers hate, and that is true
And there is a profound silence, Albert Square
Held suspended in a moment of such clarity
Of breathing in before letting go
And the speeches are the story of the city
And that poem is the story of the city too
Ringing out to say – this will not beat us
We will not be made different to each other
If you thought this would make us cower
You have got us badly wrong, so wrong

And then the bees come, in swarms
And that is a good thing too at first
Sluggish after semi-hibernation
They raise themselves from pavements
Unpeel from litter bins, gain dimensions
Shout solidarity, lead to smiling glances
You are in the story too, thanks for showing it
And they mean welcome to strangers
They really do, or we are Manchester
And they mean the heart of this city cannot be shattered
And they mean I will carry this for life

And then the wave rolls on, but we try to re-create it
In seas of flowers and spontaneous collection
Sing 'Don't Look Back in Anger' for the camera
A song where only one line carries meaning
Playing the role now, of togetherness
Performing for the worldwide networks
That flocked more to make content than to help
But maybe part of us wants to be fooled as well

The Watsons

Laura Wade

Laura Wade is an Olivier Award-winning playwright and screenwriter. Her National Theatre play *Home, I'm Darling* premiered at Theatr Clwyd in 2018 before playing at the National where it received rave reviews. It won the award for Best New Comedy at the 2019 Olivier Awards. In 2018 Laura adapted Jane Austen's unfinished novel *The Watsons* for the stage for Chichester Festival Theatre. After a successful run at the Menier Chocolate Factory, *The Watsons* was scheduled to open in the West End in 2020 at the Harold Pinter Theatre.

In 2015 Laura adapted Sarah Waters's *Tipping the Velvet* for the stage. The play premiered at the Lyric Hammersmith before transferring to the Royal Lyceum in Edinburgh. Laura's screenplay *The Riot Club*, an adaptation of her 2010 stage play *Posh*, premiered at Toronto International Film Festival 2014 and opened in cinemas in September 2014. *Posh* opened in the West End at the Duke of York's Theatre in May 2012 following a run at the Royal Court Theatre in April 2010 to sell-out audiences.

What does the word `crisis' mean to you in a theatrical sense?

A play needs to have a problem at its heart. The job of a play is to try to unpick that problem and that's something unique to theatre. We gather together to examine a crisis and consider it at length and from different perspectives than our own, in a way that real life doesn't always let us do. I remember Edward Bond giving a seminar to a group of playwrights in which he introduced us to the phrase `accident time'. I took this to mean the way time can seem to stop during a moment of crisis and you have a heightened sensory awareness – literally seconds, but it can feel like hours. In my mind, it's like the bullet time effect in The Matrix where a moment freezes and the camera can circle the characters, giving a 360-degree view. The important thing while writing is that you have to stay in that crisis, you mustn't solve it immediately – the crisis is the play. (I'm paraphrasing Edward Bond again here, but it was a very good seminar.) A play can hold us in a moment, to take the time to fully consider an idea without always having to impatiently scramble for the next event – which is why the theatre is still the place we go to think about urgent problems in our society.

How do you feel theatre has the ability to represent/respond to global crises?

I think what theatre does best is take a long view. It can look back on an event or a period after it has happened, a ruminant way of processing something. I'm slightly suspicious of rapid-response writing projects, people who ask for your `half-hour play about the corona crisis by the end of the week please'. I think to myself, I don't know what I think about it yet – and I consider it my prerogative as a playwright to take my time deciding, so you can't have that play from me until next year or the year after because that's how long it takes to percolate. (Of course you have to hope that audiences will still be interested in the idea by then – but that's also part of a playwright's job, to diagnose which of the shiny ideas in front of you is a diamond, and which is only sugar glass.)

The best plays ask more questions than they give answers. They also present things in a metaphorical or allegorical frame, where the news media is necessarily more literal. That's something to really hold onto about the theatre because it's special. We come to the auditorium to ask questions together, to look at things through metaphor, and often through a historical filter. Theatre is very good at joining things up – comparing our moment to events in the past, and thinking what can be learned about people at that time, and ourselves in the present. (Look out for a glut of plays about the bubonic plague in the next few years, then …)

Why did you pick this specific scene? What is this scene doing at this point of the play?

It's the point where the play changes from being a slick Jane Austen adaptation into an existential crisis and an exploration of both what it means to be a character, and what it means for a writer to leave a piece of work unfinished, and the characters in limbo. It's really a fulcrum; it's the point where the play starts to become itself rather than an adaption of someone else's story. For Emma it's the biggest crisis of her life. She thought her worst-case scenario was having to go back and live with her tiresome birth family, having been brought up by a wealthy aunt. She's unmarried and has no money of her own and she has to find someone to marry. So that seems like the biggest crisis in the first twenty minutes of the play, then this other one comes along which blows it out of the water because she's told she doesn't even exist. How can she deal with that? Something I like about this play is that Emma goes through all of that on stage in front of us, but every other character, even the smallest parts, learns the same thing about themselves, and they all have to process the idea that they're fictional and make peace with it or find a way to fight it.

This scene is the point where audiences were jolted out of their expectations. It's a really spare scene, just the two of them on stage, where earlier the stage was much fuller. In the first production the lighting changed subtly here, not so that you'd notice, but to bring us into a different world. The scene is also quite different in terms of its structure: it's about six or seven pages long where everything else has been rattling along quickly. Suddenly we stop and we're in 'accident time'.

How does this scene speak beyond the wider context of the play?

I think we all remember a moment where it occurs to us to think, 'Am I the only person that's real and everyone else is an actor?' or, 'Is this my dream or someone else's?' Particularly as teenagers. I was interested by how popular this play was with teenagers who came to see it: I think many hadn't yet seen something that had that kind of meta-theatrical playfulness, a play that takes itself apart. Perhaps it taps into where you are at that age, that you're existentially asking some of those big questions.

As a writer, do you feel a point of crisis is always necessary in a play to create/maintain/sustain drama?

I think that's a really interesting question. I'm very structural as a writer and not very organic. I have to do a lot of structural work before the writing can flow. So I'm quite aware as I'm writing where the crisis points in the play are, and what the graph of the story looks like.

And I think as an audience somewhere in our bones we expect to be leading up to and away from a climax. So it's probably not essential to build to that, but if you're not going to do it you have to be skilful about what else you do in order for the play to have a satisfying shape. Of course you don't only want the audience to go away satisfied – and there are good arguments for not tying things up neatly, if you want the audience to retain their feeling of anger or injustice, or leave the theatre determined to change the world. I'm interested in the fact that 'crisis' used to be a euphemism for orgasm, in a way that we use the word 'climax' now. There's something in the idea that our habitual narrative shape is actually quite a masculine or patriarchal model, in the same way that the male orgasm can be seen as quite, erm, linear. I wonder if there are 'feminine' narrative forms that we haven't properly explored yet that have a less linear and perhaps more circular form – a feminine mode that's more about little crises, mini-earthquakes or circles and less 'one big crisis' that we lead up to and then away from. We're so culturally used to the masculine form, it's absolutely everything that we've ever grown up with in terms of storytelling – it's exciting to think of new narrative shapes emerging that challenge our expectations formally, and of future writers experimenting with them while the audience runs to keep up.

When constructing a play how do you effectively boil down larger global themes that could otherwise be overwhelming for characters within 'their world' so that they can find room to resonate?

You have to find a metaphorical way to express your theme. When I was first researching the world of *Posh*, the intention was to write a big exploration of wealth and power in British society. But that's not a play until it has characters and a scenario. That's an audience watching the Olivier stage turning around endlessly with nothing on it. The point where it came alive to me was ten boys sitting around a table in a restaurant that they knew they were going to smash up at the end of the evening, and that become the suitcase into which all of the other ideas could get packed. You need that kind of a foundation, a metaphor that is rich enough so that all of the big ideas can be in the play and be properly resonant without too much crowbarring. You find the specific. If I sat down and thought 'I'm going to write the definitive play about the NHS' I'd get stuck on an image of a load of actors in white coats pushing trollies around (that Olivier revolve again). But someone somewhere is writing that play, with a brilliant and specific story at the heart of it – the brilliant consultant who has found the cure for cancer but is hamstrung by bureaucracy, for example – and there is room in that allegorical framework for lots of other ideas about the health of the nation.

What do you feel is the biggest threat to the creation of new drama and plays given the current global crisis?

Funding. We have a useful pipeline in this country: someone like me does a play in a studio theatre in Sheffield to start off with, then student theatre productions at university, then a play at the Finborough in London which is a tiny but excellent fringe venue, and from there to the Royal Court Upstairs and Soho Theatre, and eventually gets paid to write for big stages and big casts. There's a progression available and a range of theatre sizes and spaces, but if you take out parts of that chain then the chain won't work anymore (and if it's only working for people who don't need to earn money from their work, then it's only nominally working anyway). It's a rare playwright who comes out of the box with the skills ready to write for the Lyttelton or the Olivier. So that ladder is essential and we need to protect the smaller theatres, and the freelancers that work in them, or there won't be anyone ready to work in the big theatres in a few years' time.

I think we've discovered this year how much we miss the theatre and its unique liveness. There is no other way of doing it. Streaming shows (or recordings of shows) is a great way of keeping the idea of theatre alive in people's minds but perhaps the most useful thing it does is make people want to go back to the theatre in person. The lack of clear support for the industry from the government is potentially a huge crisis for the industry. It could take a very long time to recover if the right sort of help isn't available. I hope we can come back from this crisis and be a stronger, more affordable and inclusive art form in the future, and once again be a useful force in people's lives. But it's definitely going to be hard work, and I don't know how we do it without funding.

The Watsons premiered at Chichester's Festival Theatre in 2018

What happens when the writer loses the plot?

Emma Watson is nineteen and new in town. She's been cut off by her rich aunt and dumped back in the family home. Emma and her sisters must marry, fast. If not, they face poverty, spinsterhood, or worse: an eternity with their boorish brother and his awful wife.

Luckily there are plenty of potential suitors to dance with, from flirtatious Tom Musgrave to castle-owning Lord Osborne, who's as awkward as he is rich.

So far so familiar. But there's a problem: Jane Austen didn't finish the story. Who will write Emma's happy ending now?

Based on her incomplete novel, this sparklingly witty play looks under the bonnet of Jane Austen and asks: what can characters do when their author abandons them?

Lord Osborne *leaves.* **Emma** *turns back to see the* **Servant** *attempting to slink out in the other direction.*

Emma Hey!

The **Servant** *freezes, turns.*

Servant (*to herself*) *Hey*? Is that right?

Emma Is this how you behave at my brother's house?

Servant I've never been to your brother's house.

Emma You're their servant.

Servant I'm actually not.

Emma You arrived with them.

Servant At the same time, yes, technically.

Emma I don't understand, who

Servant You must know you can't marry him.

Emma Why not? And what concern is it of y

Servant You don't love him.

Emma I might come to love him later.

Servant You said to Elizabeth you'd never marry someone you didn't love.

Emma What alternative is there? A lifetime chained to my family – have you seen my family? I wasn't brought up to be poor, to be dependent on

How do you know what I said to Elizabeth?

Servant That needn't concern you right now. These are not the droids you're looking for.

Emma What?

Servant Did he say anything about loving you?

Emma He was nervous.

Servant He's an idiot, Emma. He's awkward and strange.

Emma For an aristocrat, he's not particularly strange.

Servant You want to make a man like that your hero?

Emma I'll be comfortable.

Servant You'll be miserable.

Emma Miserable in Osborne Castle?

It is large enough we need rarely be in the same room.

If I marry Lord Osborne I will live as I have been used to – plenty of servants and not worrying about the price of sugar and a horse to ride and a gallery to walk in when it's wet.

I might never have a chance this good again.

Servant You're nineteen – there'll be other offers.

Emma Nineteen is nearly twenty and twenty is nearly twenty-one and before I know it I shall be twenty-eight like Elizabeth which is nearly thirty.

Servant What if I could get you something better?

Emma *You*?

Servant Yes.

Emma What could *you* do about it?

Servant OK, look

I'm going to have to tell you.

OK, I think I'm going to have to tell you.

Emma What?

Servant I'm going to try telling you and see how it, God this is so unprofessional.

OK.

Have you ever heard of a person called Jane Austen?

Emma No.

Servant OK. Jane Austen is an author.

Emma Oh, how dreadful!

Servant Sorry?

Emma I feel so sorry for them. To be quite alone in the world. Mother might have died when I was a baby but at least we still have father. To be without any parents at all must be

Servant Not an *orphan*. An *author*. A writer.

Emma Oh. Of?

Servant Books. Great, great books.

Emma A woman?

Servant Yes. A parson's daughter, like you, but a very celebrated author – not as much as she should have been during her lifetime, but since then

Emma She isn't alive?

Servant That sort of depends where we are in time.

Emma I don't understand.

Servant The thing is – Jane Austen isn't just any author, she's *your* author.

Emma Mine?

Servant The author of all this, this world, this

This is a book – well now it's a play.

Emma A play?

She looks all around for an audience, peers out into the auditorium.

Servant Don't worry about them for now.

Jane Austen created this world but she didn't finish it.

Emma Why?

Servant Nobody knows – it happens to writers. Something interrupts you, a life event or. Something gets in the way so you put it in the bottom drawer then before you know it two hundred years have passed

Emma Two hundred years?

Servant That's a joke. Sorry, too soon.

Sometimes you just can't work out how to write something so you stop, you leave it unfinished.

And that's where I come in, because here I am, now, picking up the baton. Badly.

I'm, um, Laura.

Emma Um Laura?

Laura Laura. I'm Laura. I'm also an author. Playwright.

Emma You're a writer.

Laura Yes.

Emma Not a servant.

Laura No.

Emma And you're not Jane Austen, who isn't here.

Laura Oh I can show you.

She reaches into her pocket, pulls out a ten pound note.

She's on some of our money now, look.

She hands the note to **Emma**.

There she is. Jane Austen.

Emma *looks at the picture of Jane Austen on the note.*

Emma She looks perfectly ordinary.

Laura It's part of her charm. Though we don't really know if that's an accurate portrait.

Emma *reads the writing on the note.*

Emma *Ten pounds*? How does a servant get ten pounds?

Laura Not a servant.

Emma Aren't you frightened someone will steal it?

Laura It's not that much where I come from.

Look, the thing is, the important thing is that Jane Austen wrote this world that we're standing in. This world is a book, a story.

And you are a character in it.

Emma Someone's writing a story about me?

Laura No, this. *This* is the story. All of this here, everything.

And you're a character.

Do you understand what I'm saying? This is fiction.

And you're part of it. You're a character.

A character not a person.

Emma I'm a person, of course I

Laura No, you're a character. You're written.

Emma You mean I'm not real?

Laura No.

You're the heroine. It's your story, so that's good.

Emma Are you real?

Laura Yes.

Emma You're real but I'm not real.

Laura This is a lot to take in, I know.

Emma (*re the bank note*) Is she real?

Laura She was.

Emma This picture of a person – you're saying this picture is more real than I am.

Laura She created you. She decided what you would do, up to the point where I came in.

Emma I decide what I do.

Laura It may feel like that.

Emma So I

These words I'm saying

Laura Yes.

Emma These *thoughts*

Laura Yes.

Emma When I move my hand

Laura It's all her.

Well her first, now me.

Emma But *I'm* the one thinking, I'm

When I touch my arm I can feel it.

Laura Yes it's a good arm.

Emma Can I sit down?

Laura Yes.

Emma Is the chair real?

Laura Yes.

Emma Lucky chair.

Laura I mean, no, it's fictional but

No, sit down, you look

Emma *sits down.*

Laura This is a shock.

I'm sorry, I didn't know you could suffer. I think I thought you couldn't if you're not

Emma I don't feel like I'm not real.

Laura You're a well-written character, Jane Austen was

Emma No, this is nonsense. This is nonsense, I'm not I'm not not r

Laura Maybe you need some time to

Emma If I wasn't real I couldn't decide to walk out of this

That's what a real person would do, just walk away because you're clearly some kind of a

Lunatic or

She makes a decision, stands up, walks out.

Laura Emma.

Emma I'm walking out.

Laura OK.

She waits. After a moment she stands up, goes to the clock and winds it forward by twenty minutes.

A moment later, **Emma** *returns, mud around the hem of her skirt.*

Laura How did you get on?

Emma I walked up the lane. A little way past the house I got to the end.

There's nothing there.

Laura No, I haven't written that bit yet.

Emma I didn't know what nothing looked like before.

Laura It's just because nothing's happened there yet. We can borrow some fields off a Thomas Hardy or something

Emma I feel sick.

Laura I didn't mean to frighten you.

Emma Why did you tell me? I don't want to know.

It feels like the first time I knew what dying was. I was so small. Four, maybe. Maybe five. I asked my nanny what happens when you die – I think our cat had died or a hamster – and she told me. You're just not there anymore, you've gone. It doesn't hurt anymore because you're not there. Your body's there, but you've gone from inside it, and eventually even your body

But how does it *feel*? It doesn't feel, she said. But how does it feel not to feel? The idea that you're not anywhere, the impossibility of understanding it and really just wanting to go back to not knowing because how can you walk about when you know?

Except none of that happened, did it, because I'm not real.

Laura No, that's my memory, actually. It was my mum, I didn't have a nanny.

Emma Are all my memories yours?

Laura No, Jane's done most of it, I think.

Look, the memories aren't important, the important thing is for us to look forward, find your story. That's why I wanted to write you. You were in a kind of limbo, unfinished, but when I read you I thought you were too special to walk away from. I wanted to know what was going to happen to you and share you with people because I just thought you were *great*.

Emma Don't flatter me, this is my life

Laura OK but we've got to find a way to work together. I've never done this before either, we're going to have to work it out together so I can carry on writing you even though you know I am.

Otherwise – well, I don't know what happens otherwise.

Emma *looks at* **Laura***, thinking. A long moment.*

Margaret*,* **Elizabeth** *and* **Mrs Robert** *burst in.* **Laura** *moves away and tries to look busy.*

Margaret I'm dying with suspense, I can't bear it!

Emma What?

Mrs Robert What did he say?

Emma Who?

Mrs Robert Lord Osborne.

Elizabeth Sorry, we couldn't wait.

Margaret We saw him ride off: what happened?

Emma He asked me to marry him.

Elizabeth Oh Emma.

The Internationalist

Anne Washburn

Anne Washburn's plays include *10 Out of 12*, *Antlia Pneumatica*, *Apparition*, *The Communist Dracula Pageant*, *A Devil at Noon*, *I Have Loved Strangers*, *The Internationalist*, *The Ladies*, *Little Bunny Foo Foo*, *Mr. Burns*, *Shipwreck*, *The Small*, an adaption of *The Twilight Zone*, and transadaptations of Euripides' *Orestes* and *Iphigenia in Aulis*. Her work has been produced nationally and internationally. Awards include a Whiting Award, a Guggenheim Fellowship, an Alpert Award, a PEN/ Laura Pels Theater Award, a NYFA Fellowship, a Time Warner Fellowship, Susan Smith Blackburn Prize finalist twice, and residencies at MacDowell and Yaddo.

How do you feel theatre has the ability to represent/respond to global crises?

I think it has the ability to represent honestly how it is that we attempt to understand global crises.

Why did you pick this specific scene? What is this scene doing at this point of the play?

I'd been thinking about it a bit – that question of how we manage crisis, how we think we will manage crisis, how unaware we are, how that unawareness will bite us in the ass, the necessity of preparing for crisis, the impossibility of preparing for crisis . . . all of these questions have felt pertinent, for me at any rate, in this moment . . .

This scene takes place towards the end of the play: Lowell is an American businessman from the American branch of a company who has gone on a trip – his first real 'business trip' – to visit colleagues in the home office in a country whose language is inexplicable to him. In the middle of this trip the office is engulfed in a crisis, which no one has the time to explain to him, which seems to involve massively complicated financial transactions and to in some way involve his colleague Paul.

As a writer, do you feel a point of crisis is always necessary in a play to create/maintain/sustain drama?

I think there has to be a moment where the characters care about something; any act of caring eventually precipitates a crisis of one kind or another.

Does theatre as a form allow for a more effective exploration of crisis in terms of what can be explored, presented and communicated to an audience, in relation to other creative forms?

I've always felt like the impulse to watch theatre, to be kind of gripped by theatre, stems from our time as newly minted humans sitting around campfires in the dark with all of our antennae bristling and alert paying close attention to the other humans around us: watching for violence and power, watching for authority, watching for anger, watching for sex, hungering for kindness, yearning for love, waiting for the unexpected, watching for watchfulness – wondering who will know what first; paying attention to the circle around us, listening to the darkness behind our back; knowing we can't do equal justice to both; knowing that to spend our lives looking only into the circle means our eyes will be blinded towards what comes towards us from the dark, but you can't spend your life searching the darkness. I feel like these are the essential underlying questions of theatre and I feel like we are nothing right now if not hyper bound up in each other and watchful of each other and so in that way theatre – the gathering of humans to scrutinise each other – speaks most intimately and intensely to us right now but of course it's the form which is denied to us most absolutely.

When constructing a play how do you effectively boil down larger global themes that could otherwise be overwhelming for characters within 'their world' so that they can find room to resonate?

Oh my God, you can't. You can't effectively boil down larger global themes and honestly you shouldn't try. I think the best theatre has always been honest about our helplessness, our awe; I think it can capture our moments of partial illumination, it can certainly capture our struggle to understand.

What do you feel is the biggest threat to the creation of new drama and plays given the current global crisis? Do we need theatre now more than ever?

The fact that our breath is poison, no? Beyond that: high rent for performance and rehearsal spaces, and even crummy artist living spaces, and (in America especially) high ticket prices.

***The Internationalist* premiered at New York's Vineyard Theatre in November 2006**

Lowell goes abroad on business. He thinks he's in one of those great American films where you go to a foreign land and there's romance and adventure. However, Lowell soon discovers that he's not in one of those movies, he's in a foreign film where nothing is as it seems, where there is no clear hero and, most importantly, no subtitles.

Lost-in-translation business trips and global travel are put under the microscope in *The Internationalist*, a play of wit, romance, misunderstandings and the mysteries of communication.

The Observatory Bar:

Daylight in a shaft from above.

Lowell *turns and addresses himself to the incredibly ancient* **Bartender**.

Lowell Du aig-ast olim freet pacada tsi hul amda.

The **Bartender** *considers him quizically.*

Lowell Du aig-ast olim freet pacada tsi hul amda.

Bartender Of course, sir.

Paul *is standing over at the other end of the bar and raises a glass to him.*

Lowell Paul.

Bit of a beat.

They're looking for you. At the office.

Paul I'm sure they are.

Lowell Apparently it's urgent.

Paul Yes.

Lowell I don't know why they're looking for you, but it sounds important, I mean they're in meetings right now. They haven't been able to get hold of you.

Paul No.

Brief pause.

Lowell It really does seem important.

Paul Did you know that before it was an observatory this structure was a tower, a military tower? I suppose what you'd call a castle although with no grandeur in the way that we think about it now. This was a time when fortification was a nasty, unpleasant business, when you protected yourself at a real cost to your comfort. This would have been a narrow – well it is, you can imagine, 100 men, 200 men, imagine the latrine system, just the stench of it, the crowding. The windows, of course, are unglazed, storage space is at a minimum so firewood is precious; you spend a lot of your time freezing on your feet with the raw cold just streaming in around you. Also, I expect you have dysentery.

He holds up his glass.

It's very nice here right now. It's so quiet. Listen. Just such ordinary sounds.

A serene silence.

The pigeons scrapping about on the roof . . . you can't hear them right now. Cars.

He taps the side of the glass to indicate the liquid in it; he taps further up to indicate the heavy glass. He looks around.

What always amazes me is that the future will look back to *this* time and find it exactly as barbaric. There's no doubt. I'm a cynical civilized man so of course I think our life is shit, and very badly managed, and that our ideals are hypocritical and deadly, but civilized men always have without ever seeing into the heart of it, never knowing what, precisely, will amuse the future . . .

What does the future see? Right now?

We're primitives, you and I, we have a big 'I am a boob' sign pasted to our backs; we're going to go down in history as chumps; we have no way of knowing why.

Of course the future will itself be judged, just as condescendingly.

Lowell I don't believe in the future.

Paul No? You think these are end times.

Lowell Yes. Don't you?

Paul It's never been the end of time before. Of *a* time. But not time itself.

Lowell Any day now I expect to be duking it out on a post-apocalyptic rubble heap for a woman.

Paul *half coughs and almost spits out his drink.*

Lowell You wouldn't think, right? But who knows. I might make out alright. It's hard to say what's going to be valuable, who will come out on top. Thank you.

He's received his drink. A martini, with an olive. He drinks half of it at once.

I'll need to invent a different past. A tougher one. I'm sure everyone will anyway. Paul, I can't say that I haven't seen you.

Paul It's alright. You can say that I had a gun – I do, although I'm not going to wave it around. I did remember the gun? (*He opens the briefcase which has been sitting on the floor near him.*) Yes. It's only a sentimental gun but it will make for a better story and it *is* loaded so you couldn't have stopped me by force even if it had occurred to you to try – and it didn't. By the time you make a phone call: what I was saying about this structure is that there are ways out of it. I'll be gone before anyone arrives. I'll be out of the city by nightfall. I'll be out of the country by dawn. And I'll be where I'm going the day after that.

Beat.

Lowell Paul. (. . .) What did you do?

Paul Something really elegant. I think you'll appreciate it, when they piece it together. It was probably the wrong decision. In the past week, as I've waited for my, uh, machineries to engage I can't tell you how precious my life here has seemed to me. The ordinariness. And my friends. They are a desperately imperfect people, nitwits actually, a lot of them, and they don't provide everything I need and they fail me with their inadequacies. But in the past few days when I've been with them, I look at them: I know the way I'm going to remember them: it's going to be like a movie, like a dreadful movie: gold light and slow motion, always set in the spring, with flower petals showering down in the rain and all of their virtues, their kindnesses, their moments of wit and insight, all of sort of parading around me. They're going to haunt me. For the rest of my life. Do you know that you are the last person I will have ever met who I will not lie to? As a matter of course. At the moment I feel such tenderness for you. Such pleasure that we were colleagues, however briefly. Such respect.

He laughs at that. Polishes off his drink.

I hope you enjoy your time here.

He picks up his briefcase and exits.

Permissions and Copyright

Adler & Gibb

Barber Shop Chronicles

A History of Falling Things

Lions and Tigers

A Museum in Baghdad

Emilia
First published by Oberon Books Ltd 2018. Copyright © Morgan Lloyd Malcolm, 2018

X
First published by Methuen Drama 2016. Copyright © Alistair McDowall, 2016

An Adventure
First published in Great Britain by Methuen Drama 2018. Copyright © Vinay Patel, 2018

The Effect
First published by Methuen Drama 2012. Copyright © Lucy Prebble, 2012

The Pitchfork Disney
First published in Great Britain by Methuen Drama 1991. Copyright © Philip Ridley, 1991

Where Do We Live
First published in Great Britain by Methuen Publishing Limited 2002. Copyright © Christopher Shinn, 2002